desserts 4 today

FLAVORFUL DESSERTS
with just
FOUR INGREDIENTS

Abigail Johnson Dodge

The Taunton Press

The Taunton Press
Inspiration for hands-on living®

The Taunton Press, Inc., 63 South Main Street, PO Box 5506, Newtown, CT 06470-5506
email: tp@taunton.com

Editor: Carolyn Mandarano
Copy editor: Li Agen
Indexer: Heidi Blough
Cover design: Kimberly A. Adis
Interior design: Kimberly A. Adis
Layout: Amy Griffin
Photographer: Kate Sears
Food stylist: Suzette Kaminski
Prop stylist: Pam Morris

The following names/manufacturers appearing in *Desserts 4 Today* are trademarks:

Frangelico®, Ghirardelli®, Glad®, Gold Medal®, Guittard®, King Arthur®, KitchenAid®, M&M's® Minis®, Microplane®, Moscato d'Asti®, Nutella®, Oreo®, Pyrex®, Scharffen Berger®, Sugar in the Raw®, Sunbeam®, Tupperware®, Ziploc®

Library of Congress Cataloging-in-Publication Data

Dodge, Abigail Johnson.
  Desserts 4 today : flavorful desserts with just four ingredients / Abigail Johnson Dodge.
      p. cm.
  title: Desserts for today
  title: Desserts four today
  Includes index.
  ISBN 978-1-60085-294-7
  1. Desserts. 2. Quick and easy cooking. I. Title. II. Title: Desserts for today. III. Title: Desserts four today.

  TX773.D626 2010
  641.8'6--dc22
                              2010020854

Printed in the United States of America

10 9 8 7 6 5 4 3 2 1

For Alex and Tierney,
I am blessed in many ways but none more than with the gift of you both. Thank you for filling my kitchen, home, and heart with inspiration, laughter, and love.

acknowledgments

In the course of my baking years, my friends, colleagues, editors, readers, and gifted chefs have inspired, encouraged, and supported me in more ways than I can mention. It is with a full heart and a grateful soul that I thank them for their contributions to this book.

Sending my warmest thanks to my pal Amy Albert for her constant friendship, advice, and support during the birth of this project and beyond.

Honesty and hard work is important in this business, and I thank Stacey Glick, my stellar agent, for always telling it like it is and pushing me to do better.

The Test Kitchen: Claire Van de Berghe is not only head of my test kitchen but also a trusted friend and colleague. I can't imagine doing a project without her and I hope I never do. Thanks to Ann Mileti and Jennifer Smith (and their families), who tested and tasted endless versions of these recipes.

The Fam: Chris and the kids (+ 3 dogs…don't ask), my brother Tim, and countless random victims graciously and patiently tasted and tasted and tasted. Thanks guys for your love, discerning taste buds, and critiques, and for washing more than your share of dishes, pots, and pans.

In many ways, The Taunton Press has been my home for over 16 years and I'm grateful for their belief in me throughout the years. Carolyn Mandarano is one rock-star editor. Thank you, Carolyn, for being creative, flexible, direct, and smart but, most of all, thank you for taking this book under your wing. It was my pleasure to work with you. Thanks to the all-star design and production team for working your magic on this project. Kim Adis, Carol Singer, Katy Binder, and Amy Griffin created the stunning and unique look and layout of this book—gorgeous! And, last but never least, Li Agen is not only a longtime friend and trusted colleague, but she's also a goddess of a copy editor.

Thanks to photographer Kate Sears, food stylist Suzette Kaminski, and prop stylist Pam Morris for pooling their monster-sized talent to create lush, amazing photos that bring the recipes to life.

My deepest thanks to Laurie Buckle, Rebecca Freedman, Scott Phillips, Jennifer Armentrout, Sarah Breckenridge, and the entire staff of *Fine Cooking* magazine and www.FineCooking.com for your continued support and inspirational work.

Richard Lerner, from Aresel Marketing, continues to guide and manage my Web site. I hear his work with me might have him up for sainthood sooner rather than later.

I'm honored and proud to be one part of the star-studded group that has created this book. Thank you.

contents

4 is the magic number

I designed this book to be a straightforward, no-nonsense collection of recipes with tips, hints, and variations to make dessert not only a possibility but also a probability in your life. Before diving into the recipes, take a moment to read through the following pages. I've taken a new approach to presenting these recipes so they're simple and fun to make. I also share my thoughts on stocking the perfect pantry, plus I'll suggest a few key pieces of equipment—large and small—to have on hand, along with some helpful hints for getting the most from your ingredients.

4 STARTERS

The recipes here are not complicated or fussy and take a modern approach in their taste. They are presented in a user-friendly way to help dessert making be as much a part of your cooking life as pasta, burgers, and baked potatoes.

Ingredients are listed first and the amount second. This way, you will know immediately if you have what you need to get going. You'll find that many of the ingredients are sitting in your pantry, fridge, or freezer. With an emphasis on fresh ingredients, these recipes deliver intriguing and flavorful results.

Flavor is the name of the game. Change things up by trying one of the variations I give in the "Switch-Ins" section of each recipe. These suggestions encourage you to think beyond your familiar flavor pairings as well as offer options for swapping ingredients that you don't have on hand, don't care for, or, in the case of fruit, aren't ripe or in season. Be adventurous with your choices, with the Switch-Ins as your guide. In the case of fresh fruit, use the ripest in-season fruit you can. And if the primary fruit doesn't look so good, swap in something similar, keeping in mind the type and texture of the original fruit called for in a recipe.

"Gussy It Up" sidebars offer suggestions for extra finishing touches for when you have the time and interest. Some options are as quick as a dusting of sugar; other times, I'll steer you to short, easy-to-follow recipes in Add-Ons (page 178). All of these additions maximize the flavor and texture of the ingredients to provide another layer of taste and sophistication.

"Tech Talk" and **"Change It Up"** highlight an alternative technique or method specific to the recipe at hand. These sections not only provide some tricks and tips that will help you along the way but also offer more options so that you really can bring dessert back into your life.

4 SIMPLE STEPS TO SUCCESS

To make the most of the recipes, follow these 4 simple steps to ensure your sweet success.

Choose your dessert

I've divided the recipes into 5 main groups: Cookies, Creamy, Frozen, Fruit, and Pastry. Turn to the section that intrigues you and page through the recipe titles before selecting one. Better yet, leaf through all the sections—you never know what irresistible dessert might catch your eye and tickle your taste buds.

Read the recipe

Begin by checking the ingredients. I've listed them ahead of the amount so you'll know immediately if you have them on hand. Next, read the recipe completely and check Essentials (page 181) if you have any questions *before* you begin.

Measure carefully and follow the directions

Using the appropriate measuring cups—metal for dry ingredients (and semi-solids, like sour cream) and glass for liquids—measuring correctly, and then following the directions will ensure consistent and delicious results.

Pay attention to the doneness test and use the timing as a guide

Directions will offer sensory clues to help you know when to move onto the next step or when you are finished. The timing is a suggested window but, depending on your equipment, kitchen and oven temperature, and ingredients, it might take a bit longer or a bit shorter.

4 OTHER REMINDERS

Give yourself permission to substitute

Swapping in other ingredients is part of the fun but, to some, it feels like breaking the rules. These substitutions give you flavor and ingredient flexibility in case you don't have exactly what the recipe is calling for or if you feel like experimenting with a new or unusual ingredient. I encourage you to taste as you cook and modify the flavorings to your taste. If you'd like more mint in your fruit compote or more rum in your sabayon, just add more in small increments and make a note of the amount you like in the margin for the next time. Break some rules—permission granted.

Select top-quality, affordable ingredients

Use the best ingredients your budget can support. With only four ingredients in a recipe, each one needs to be stellar or the taste will suffer and you'll be disappointed.

Embrace seasonal fruits

There's no better way to be creative (see rule #1) and have fun than by using the ripest, in-season, local fruits. Check out the produce at your local farmers' markets, pick-your-own farms, and greenmarkets; even better, consider joining a CSA (Community Supported Agriculture). "Going local" is a great way to support your community and get some of the best regional varieties.

Have fun!

Numerology dabblers know that the number 4 represents, among other things, structure, stability, and balance—heck, even if it's not about baking, I'm all for having these traits in my life. In addition, the recipes are designed to be stress-free and easy without a heavy investment in time, patience, and resources. These recipes will make people happy and will turn even the most novice baker into a rock-star pastry chef.

STOCKING UP YOUR PANTRY

Having a variety of these ingredients stowed in your fridge, freezer, and pantry will guarantee an all-star dessert. By no means are you expected to have every item I've listed—just be sure to have at least one from each category tucked into your kitchen arsenal so you can "dessert" at a moment's notice.

All-purpose flour. There are many different varieties and brands of flour on the market, but for these recipes you need only stock all-purpose, white. I like King Arthur® and Gold Medal® brands and, unless you are a big-time baker, you need only a small bag, about 1 pound, on hand. Store it in an airtight container to keep it fresh and bug-free.

Chocolate. I like my chocolate to be about 60% to 62% chocolate solids. Most brands will call this "bittersweet" but not all, so double-check the label. For example, Scharffen Berger®'s (one of my favorites) "semisweet" is 62% chocolate, which is the same percentage as Ghirardelli®'s bittersweet. The higher-percentage chocolate will give a stronger, more bitter flavor. For chips, I like Guittard® and Ghirardelli brands. There are many bittersweet and semisweet chocolate varieties out there, so I encourage you sample often and make note of your favorites.

Dairy. Use only **unsalted butter.** This butter is fresher than the salted version and allows you to control the amount of salt added to your recipe. **Large eggs** are the rule. Switching in different sizes will yield inconsistent results. **Half-and-half** and **heavy cream** are not interchangeable, but you can buy them in small quantities and they'll keep for a few weeks. Unless otherwise mentioned, use only **whole, 2%, or 1% milk.**

Flavorings. Use only **pure extracts** and pass over the subpar imitation varieties. Vanilla and almond are two that I always have on hand. Small jars of **ground spices** like cinnamon, ginger, and nutmeg will taste vibrant for up to 6 months. After that, I'd urge you to crack open a new container or your dessert's flavor may be limp and weak. Good-quality **maple syrup,** like Grade B or Grade A dark amber, is a strong flavor as well as sweetener.

Jarred goodness. Tuck a jar or two of your favorite jam or preserves into the cabinet, along with citrus curd and dulce de leche. They will deliver big flavor boosts to your desserts.

Nuts. Keep a small stash of your favorite nuts in a heavy-duty container or zip-top bag in the freezer to keep them tasting fresh. Unless otherwise indicated, nuts are easily swappable. Toast 'em when directed, as it heightens the nuts' flavor.

Premades. There are many high-quality prepared foods available in grocery and gourmet shops, so take advantage of these timesavers. I keep a pint or two of my favorite **ice cream** flavors in my freezer, along with a box of **pie dough** and/or **puff pastry, ready-to-serve tartlet shells,** and a **vanilla pound cake. Cookies** and **cookie crusts** are also staples.

Salt. I always add at least a pinch of salt to every dessert recipe, and you should, too. Use table salt—not coarse ones like kosher or sea—because the grains are finer and dissolve faster and more evenly.

Sweeteners. **Granulated sugar, light and/or dark brown sugar, and confectioners' sugar** (powdered sugar) are the most common. Unless otherwise indicated, light and dark brown sugars are interchangeable, with the dark variety lending a slightly stronger molasses flavor and darker color to your dessert. Stow all sugar in airtight containers (I use Tupperware®). Have a jar of **honey** tucked into your pantry. A number of flavors are widely available; check your local sources for artisan varieties, too.

GUIDELINES FOR USING FRUIT

Fruit. **Fresh, ripe fruit** is the star ingredient in many recipes. Choose ripe, seasonal fruit and use it quickly. Checking for ripeness is dependant on the type of fruit you're using, but here are some general guidelines.

Tree fruit (pears, apricots, peaches, plums, nectarines). Choose firm but not hard fruit. The shoulders (just below the stem) should give slightly when pressed. Give the fruit a good sniff—the more fragrant, the better the taste.

Berries and cherries. Look for firm, plump fruit with bright coloring, and avoid any with a hint of mold or moisture.

Tropical fruit (mangos, papayas, bananas, kiwi). Choose firm but not hard fruit and avoid any with bruises or wrinkles. Bananas and papayas are ready to eat when yellow or as directed in the recipe.

Citrus. Select heavy, firm fruit without soft spots or bruises. The rind's color should be vibrant, and the fruit should have a strong citrus fragrance.

Individually quick-frozen fruit. IQF fruit is widely available, and while not a substitute for what's on your counter, it will whip up into some terrific recipes. You can make your own IQF fruit in a snap. Arrange rinsed and dried berries and pitted cherries in a single layer on a baking sheet or large plate lined with parchment, plastic wrap, or foil for easy clean up. Freeze until very firm, then transfer to freezer bags or containers and keep frozen until ready to use or for up to 6 months.

Dried fruit. There are also now vast varieties of **dried fruits** available nationwide. Choose fruits with vibrant colors and plump flesh and avoid packages where you can't see the fruit.

TOP 10 EQUIPMENT ESSENTIALS

Fancy, expensive machines aren't necessary for these recipes, but a few well-chosen items will make desserts flow from your kitchen. As with the ingredients, be choosy and purchase the best equipment your budget can support.

Baking and cookie sheets. These are not the same thing! A baking sheet (jellyroll pan) has four 1-inch-high sides. Have one on hand—it's great for toasting nuts. For cookie baking, purchase sheets with one raised edge. The edge allows for easy handling, and the remaining rimless edges allow for even cooking. Choose both types made from heavy-duty, shiny (not dark) aluminum.

Baking pans. As with other equipment, select heavy-duty, affordable baking pans and only in the quantity that your space permits. Here are a few to have on hand: muffin pans (mini and regular); Pyrex® 8½ x 4½-inch loaf, 9-inch pie plate, and 8-inch-square pans; and 8-inch round cake pan.

Blender or food processor. It's close to impossible for me to choose between these two power tools. They both have a place in my kitchen. That said, a food processor is more versatile. For the most flexibility, choose one that has a variety of work bowl sizes.

Electric mixer (hand-held or stand). Everyone needs one but you don't have to break the bank to get a good-quality model. If you have the counter space, I urge you to buy a freestanding mixer. My KitchenAid® has been working hard for over 30 years, and Sunbeam® makes a great mixer, too. If a hand-held mixer fits your space and budget restrictions, look for one with a comfortable handle, sturdy beater blades, and multiple speeds.

Knives. Yup, even bakers need a few good knives. I suggest you stow a paring knife, a chef's knife, and a serrated (bread) knife in your drawer or block and keep them sharp. A dull knife causes more injuries than a sharp one, and it will only slow your work. I take my knives to my local butcher when they need a new edge or just a quick professional sharpening.

Measuring tools. You need both glass and metal. Glass (Pyrex) measures are for all liquids, and metal measuring cups are for dry ingredients and thicker creamy items like yogurt, crème fraîche, and mascarpone. You'll also need at least one set of standard measuring spoons.

Mixing bowls. You'll need at least one of each: small, medium, large. I prefer Pyrex heatproof bowls for mixing. They can go in the microwave, on top of simmering water, in the dishwasher, and, heck, they can even go in the oven. Metal bowls are good, too. They're lighter weight than the Pyrex but aren't microwave-safe. Stay away from plastic bowls, as they aren't as sturdy, they stain easily, and they can hold onto strong odors.

Nonstick liners. Used to line cookie sheets, baking sheets, and pans, there are two nonstick varieties that I recommend—silicone-coated fiberglass baking mats and kitchen parchment—and many brands are available of each. All share common goals: keep the baked goods from sticking and make clean up easy-breezy. Unless otherwise noted, they are interchangeable. Silicone baking mats come in many sizes and are sturdy, washable, and reusable. Kitchen parchment (also called baking paper) is silicone-coated paper that can withstand oven temperatures up to 450°F. Available in many forms, I find the flat sheets the easiest to work with, and they can be cut to fit any pan. P.S.: Waxed paper is **not** a substitute!

Strainers. Most likely, you already have a **large colander** in your cupboard. It's what you use to drain your cooked pasta and rinse and drain your fruit. I also recommend having a medium-size, **fine-mesh sieve** for straining liquids and purées.

Wire racks. If I'm baking just one sheet of cookies or one small baking dish, I'll occasionally let my cold cooktop stand in as a cooling rack. But you can't always count on a cold cooktop or only needing room for one hot-from-the-oven item, so have one or two large racks at the ready. They are inexpensive and will last a lifetime.

TOP 10 SMALL, INEXPENSIVE GADGETS WORTH HAVING

Microplane® zester. While they come in a variety of shapes and sizes, I like a wide, stainless-steel blade with very small and extremely sharp holes or rasps for finely grating citrus zest or fresh ginger. A rubber-coated handle keeps this very sharp tool in control.

Offset spatula. The metal blade of this handy tool jogs out from its handle at about a 45-degree angle and then continues out to a flat, dull blade. I have long and short ones in my drawer. Nothing is better for spreading a soft dough, creamy filling, batter, frosting, or glaze.

Pastry brush. Choose natural-bristled brushes with sturdy handles. I suggest having a small one for brushing water or egg wash on pastry. A medium one is ideal for brushing away excess flour from dough—a luxury, not a necessity.

Peeler. The Y- or U-shaped with a ceramic blade is my peeler of choice because it affords the most control.

Rolling pin. My pin of choice is a straight wooden cylinder without handles or slightly tapered ends. In a pinch, a straight-sided wine bottle, carefully handled, will also get the job done.

Ruler. I know I sound like a control freak, but I want your results to be the same as mine. Using a ruler is the only way you'll know that your pan or pastry dough is the same size that's called for in the recipes. I suggest a wooden or plastic ruler at least 12 to 20 inches long.

Silicone, heatproof spatulas. These "rubber" spatulas are the newest and most durable on the market.

Thermometers. Make sure you're cooling, freezing, and baking at the correct temps by investing in one thermometer each for the fridge, the freezer, and the oven. I think the mercury-filled ones are the most accurate.

Timer. Sure, your oven or microwave has one, but a separate, freestanding timer is great to carry with you if you have to leave the kitchen—it's even better if it clips to your shirt or sweater.

Whisks. Wire whisks are great for blending ingredients. I suggest having a small and a medium one on hand.

I have
long held that cookies
have medicinal qualities. OK, maybe
"medicinal" is too strong a word and quite possibly mis-
leading, but there's something soothing and calming about biting
into buttery, rich cookies of all sizes, shapes, and flavors. Whether you
like your cookies soft, chewy, crispy, or sandwiched, there are plenty here that
will put a smile on any face. ❈ To make quick work of dropping cookie batter onto
sheets, invest in a mini ice cream scooper, about 1½ inches in diameter. Not only will

cookies

you buzz through cookie production, but your baked cookies will be uniform in size and
shape and bake evenly. ❈ Most recipes in this section are baked on one cookie sheet
on an oven rack set in the middle of the oven. If you are using two sheets, adjust
one oven rack in the top third of the oven and a second one in the bottom
third. Bake the cookies as directed, switching and rotating the sheets
about halfway through the baking time. ❈ Finally, unless otherwise directed, set the hot cookie sheet on a rack to cool
for 5 minutes and transfer the cookies to a
rack to cool completely.

Flourless Chocolate Mousse Bites

MAKES 12 BITES

chocolate
(bittersweet or
semisweet),
2 ounces, chopped

unsalted butter
2 tablespoons

granulated sugar
3 tablespoons, divided

large eggs
2, separated and divided

1. Heat the oven to 325°F. Line a 12-cup mini muffin pan with paper or foil liners and lightly coat with cooking spray.

2. Put the chocolate and butter in a medium, heatproof bowl and heat in a microwave or over simmering water until melted. Whisk until smooth and blended. Add 2 tablespoons of the sugar and whisk until blended. Set aside.

3. Put 1 egg white (discard the remaining egg white) in a small bowl. Beat with an electric mixer on medium speed until foamy. Increase the speed to medium high and beat until the whites hold soft peaks. Continue beating while gradually adding the remaining 1 tablespoon sugar. Beat until medium-firm, glossy peaks form.

4. Add the 2 egg yolks to the chocolate mixture and whisk until well blended. Using a rubber spatula, fold the beaten white into the chocolate mixture until well blended. Spoon the batter into the prepared muffin tins.

5. Bake until the bites are puffed and a pick comes out with wet crumbs, about 14 minutes. Set on a rack to cool completely. Serve immediately or cover and store at room temperature for up to 2 days.

Switch-Ins
In place of the granulated sugar, switch in the following:
• brown sugar, 3 tablespoons

Gussy It Up
Add one or more of the following to the butter-chocolate mixture:
• ground cinnamon, ¼ teaspoon
• chopped peanuts, 2 tablespoons
• crystallized ginger, finely chopped, 1 tablespoon
• dried cherries, finely chopped, 2 tablespoons
• toffee bits, 2 tablespoons

Grown-Up Chocolate Bourbon Balls

MAKES 24 BOURBON BALLS

chocolate
(bittersweet or semisweet),
6 ounces, chopped

unsalted butter
6 tablespoons, cut up

bourbon
3 to 4 tablespoons

crisp vanilla wafer cookies
finely crushed,
2 cups (7 ounces), divided

1. Have ready a large, flat plate and make room in the fridge.

2. Heat the chocolate and butter in a medium saucepan or in the microwave in a medium bowl until just melted. Add the bourbon and stir until smooth and blended. Pour in $1\frac{1}{2}$ cups of the crushed cookies (save the remainder for coating). Stir until well blended.

3. Refrigerate until chilled and firm enough to shape, stirring frequently, about 20 minutes (for faster chilling, pop the bowl in the freezer).

4. Pour the remaining $\frac{1}{2}$ cup crushed cookies into a small bowl. Shape the dough into $1\frac{1}{4}$-inch balls. Roll each ball in the remaining cookies until lightly coated and set on the plate. Cover and refrigerate until ready to serve or for up to 4 days. Serve slightly chilled.

Switch-Ins
In place of the bourbon, switch in one of the following:
• orange juice or water, 3 tablespoons
• other liqueur (dark rum, amaretto, orange liqueur, Frangelico®, etc.),
  3 to 4 tablespoons

In place of the crushed vanilla wafer cookies, switch in one or a combination of two of the following to equal 2 cups:
• graham cracker crumbs
• gingersnap cookie crumbs
• chocolate wafer crumbs
• amaretti cookie crumbs
• finely chopped nuts (hazelnuts, pecans, pistachios, walnuts, almonds, macadamias), lightly toasted

Gussy It Up
Roll the bourbon balls in chopped pistachios instead of cookie crumbs.

Flaky Cinnamon Sugar Crisps

MAKES 30 COOKIES

granulated sugar
⅔ cup

ground cinnamon
1¾ teaspoons

premade pie dough
1 sheet, thawed

unsalted butter
4 tablespoons, melted

1. Heat the oven to 375°F. Line 1 large cookie sheet with a nonstick liner. Put the sugar and cinnamon in a small bowl, stir until blended, and set aside.

2. Carefully unfold or unroll the pie dough. Using a rolling pin, roll out the dough into a 12-inch round. Using a 2-inch round cookie cutter, cut out rounds. Working with one round at a time, dip the rounds into the melted butter, allowing the excess to drip off. Dredge both sides of the round in the cinnamon sugar, patting to coat both sides well.

3. Arrange the rounds on the prepared cookie sheet about ½ inch apart. Gather together the dough scraps and reroll to about ⅛-inch thickness. Cut out more rounds, dip in butter, dredge in cinnamon sugar, and arrange on the baking sheet.

4. Bake until puffed and golden brown, about 12 minutes. Set on a rack to cool completely. Serve warm or cover and store at room temperature for up to 2 days.

Switch-Ins
In place of the granulated sugar, switch in the following:
• brown sugar, ⅔ cup, firmly packed

Gussy It Up
Stir ⅓ cup finely chopped walnuts or pecans into the cinnamon sugar.

Change It Up
In place of the round cookie cutters, use any different 2-inch shape you like.

Espresso Cut-Out Snaps

MAKES 24 COOKIES

instant espresso powder
¾ teaspoon

unsalted butter
8 tablespoons, at room temperature

brown sugar
½ cup, firmly packed

all-purpose flour
1¼ cups

1. Heat the oven to 350°F. Line 2 cookie sheets with nonstick liners. Put the instant espresso powder and 1 teaspoon water in a small bowl; stir until dissolved.

2. Put the butter and brown sugar in a medium bowl. Beat with an electric mixer on low speed until smooth and blended, about 1 minute. Pour in the dissolved espresso and beat until blended. Add the flour. Beat on medium-low speed until just blended, about 1 minute.

3. Shape the dough into a flat disk and place on a large piece of plastic wrap and cover with another piece of plastic. Using a rolling pin, roll out the dough to ⅛- to ¼-inch thickness, lifting and repositioning the plastic wraps as you roll. Using a 2½-inch cookie cutter, cut out rounds.

4. Arrange the cut outs on the prepared cookie sheets about 1 inch apart. Gather together the dough scraps and reroll to about ⅛-inch thickness. Cut out more rounds.

5. Bake until the tops look dry, about 14 minutes. Set on a rack to cool completely. Cover and store at room temperature for up to 3 days.

Switch-Ins
In place of the espresso powder, switch in the following:
• instant coffee granules, 1 teaspoon

In place of the brown sugar, switch in the following:
• granulated sugar, ½ cup

Gussy It Up
• Add ½ teaspoon ground cinnamon to the butter-sugar mixture along with the dissolved espresso.
• Decorate with Chocolate Drizzle (page 178).

Nutella Fudge Brownies

MAKES 12 BROWNIES

Nutella® spread
½ cup

large egg
1

all-purpose flour
5 tablespoons

hazelnuts
chopped,
¼ cup

1. Heat the oven to 350°F. Line a 12-cup mini muffin pan with paper or foil liners.

2. Put the Nutella and egg in a medium bowl and whisk until smooth and well blended. Add the flour and whisk until blended.

3. Spoon the batter into the prepared muffin tins (about ¾ full) and sprinkle with the chopped hazelnuts.

4. Bake until a pick comes out with wet, gooey crumbs, 11 to 12 minutes. Set on a rack to cool completely. Serve immediately or cover and store at room temperature for up to 3 days.

Switch-Ins
In place of the hazelnuts, switch in one of the following:
• ground cinnamon, ¼ teaspoon (add with the flour)
• peanuts, chopped, ¼ cup

Sparkling Cocoa Drops

MAKES 22 COOKIES

granulated sugar
1 cup, divided

unsalted butter
8 tablespoons, at room
temperature

**unsweetened cocoa
powder**
⅓ cup

all-purpose flour
1 cup

1. Heat the oven to 350°F. Line 2 cookie sheets with nonstick liners. Put ¼ cup of the sugar in a small ramekin or bowl and set aside.

2. Put the butter, the remaining ¾ cup sugar, and the cocoa powder in a medium bowl. Beat with an electric mixer on low speed until smooth and blended, about 1 minute. Add the flour. Beat on medium-low speed until just blended, about 1 minute.

3. Using your hands, press and roll the dough into 1-inch balls (about 1 tablespoon firmly packed dough). Roll the balls in the reserved sugar and arrange on the prepared cookie sheets about 1½ inches apart. Using the palm of one hand, press down into each mound to flatten slightly (to about ½ inch thick). Don't worry if the edges crack a bit.

4. Bake until the tops look dry, 11 to 12 minutes. Don't overcook or the cookies will be dry. Let the cookies sit for 5 minutes and then transfer them to a rack to cool completely. Serve immediately or cover and store at room temperature for up to 2 days.

Switch-Ins
In place of the granulated sugar, switch in the following:
• brown sugar, ⅔ cup, firmly packed

Gussy It Up
Add one or more of the following to the sugar-butter-cocoa mixture:
• ground cinnamon, ½ teaspoon
• crystallized ginger, finely chopped, ¼ cup
• orange zest, finely grated, 2 teaspoons
• dried cherries, chopped, ¼ cup

Chocolate Caramel Nut Bark

SERVES 6 TO 8

chocolate
(bittersweet or semisweet),
4 ounces, melted

caramels
6 small squares,
unwrapped

slivered almonds
¼ cup, toasted

fleur de sel
pinch

1. Line 1 large cookie sheet with a nonstick liner and make room in the fridge.

2. Pour the melted chocolate onto the center of the liner. Using an offset spatula, spread the chocolate evenly into a 7½-inch round. Put the caramels in a small ramekin and add 1½ teaspoons water. Melt in the microwave until boiling, about 45 seconds. Using a small spatula, stir until well blended and smooth. Drizzle the very hot caramel in a zigzag pattern over the top of the chocolate and lightly swirl the two together with the tip of a knife.

3. Sprinkle the toasted almonds over the top, pressing gently into the chocolate and caramel. Sprinkle the fleur de sel over the top. Slide the sheet into the fridge and chill until firm, about 20 minutes, or for up to 2 days. Cut into jagged pieces and serve cold.

Switch-Ins

In place of the bittersweet or semisweet chocolate, switch in one of the following:
• white or milk chocolate, 4 ounces, melted

In place of the caramels and water, switch in the following:
• white chocolate, 2 ounces, melted

In place of the slivered almonds, switch in one of the following:
• dried apricots, chopped, ¼ cup
• dried sweet cherries, chopped, ¼ cup
• sweetened shredded coconut, ¼ cup, toasted
• chopped nuts (hazelnuts, pecans, pistachios, walnuts, macadamias), ¼ cup, toasted

Gussy It Up

Drizzle the assembled bark with 1 ounce (3 tablespoons) melted white chocolate before refrigerating.

Tech Talk
Fleur de sel is an artisan sea salt from the Guérande region in France. Known as a "finishing salt," it has a slightly crunchy texture and it dissolves quickly on the tongue, giving each bite of bark an intense, slightly sweet hit of saltiness.

Toasted Pistachio Crisps

MAKES 28 COOKIES

unsalted butter
8 tablespoons, at room temperature

confectioners' sugar
¾ cup

all-purpose flour
1¼ cups

pistachios
chopped and toasted, ⅔ cup

1. Put the butter and confectioners' sugar in a medium bowl. Beat with an electric mixer on low speed until smooth and blended, about 1 minute. Add the flour and pistachios and beat on medium-low speed until just blended, about 1 minute.

2. Shape the dough into a 7-inch round or square log. Wrap in plastic wrap and refrigerate until firm, about 2 hours or for up to 2 days. For faster chilling, pop the dough into the freezer until firm, about 30 minutes.

3. Heat the oven to 350°F. Line 2 cookie sheets with nonstick liners.

4. Cut the log into ¼-inch slices and arrange on the prepared cookie sheets about 1½ inches apart. Bake until the edges are golden brown, 13 to 15 minutes. Let the cookies sit for 5 minutes and then transfer them to a rack to cool completely. Serve immediately or cover and store at room temperature for up to 3 days.

Switch-Ins
In place of the chopped pistachios, switch in one of the following:
• sliced almonds, ¾ cup, toasted
• chopped pecans, ⅔ cup, toasted

Gussy It Up
Top with Chocolate Drizzle (page 178).

Soft Butterscotch Fantails

MAKES 12 COOKIES

unsalted butter
8 tablespoons, at room temperature

brown sugar
firmly packed,
2/3 cup, divided

yolk from large egg
1

all-purpose flour
1 cup + more for dusting

1. Heat the oven to 350°F. Using cooking spray, lightly grease a 9¹/₂-inch tart pan with a removable bottom.

2. Put the butter and ¹/₂ cup of the brown sugar in a medium bowl. Beat with an electric mixer on low speed until blended, about 1 minute. Add the egg yolk and beat until blended. Add the flour and beat on medium-low speed until just blended, about 1 minute.

3. Using your fingertips, pat the dough into the bottom of the prepared tart pan to make an even layer. If the dough is sticky, lightly coat your fingers with additional flour. Sprinkle the remaining brown sugar around the outside edge of the dough.

4. Bake until golden brown and the dough begins to pull away from the sides of the pan, about 26 minutes. Set on a rack and let cool completely. Remove the outer ring and cut into 12 wedges. Serve immediately or cover and store at room temperature for up to 2 days.

Switch-Ins
In place of the brown sugar, switch in the following:
• granulated maple sugar, 2/3 cup, divided

Gussy It Up
Do one or more of the following:
• Add ½ cup chopped walnuts or pecans to the batter along with the flour.
• Dip the pointed tips of the baked and cooled wedges into Chocolate Drizzle (page 178) or melted white chocolate and set on a rack until the chocolate hardens.
• Dust the tops of the baked and cooled wedges with confectioners' sugar.
• Serve with your favorite flavor of ice cream.

Big Orange Molasses Sandwiches

MAKES 8 SANDWICH COOKIES

cream cheese
4 ounces, at room temperature

confectioners' sugar
1⅓ cups

orange zest
finely grated,
2 teaspoons

molasses cookies
soft 3 inch,
16

1. Put the cream cheese, confectioners' sugar, and orange zest in a medium bowl. Beat with an electric mixer on low speed until blended, about 30 seconds. Increase the speed to high and beat until well blended and very smooth.

2. Arrange 8 cookies, top side down, on the counter. Portion the cream cheese mixture evenly onto the center of the cookies (about 2½ table-spoons each). Position the remaining cookies, top side up, on the cream. Gently press the cookies together to spread the filling to the edges.

3. Wrap the cookies in plastic wrap and refrigerate until the cream is firm, about 30 minutes or for up to 2 days. Serve chilled.

Switch-Ins
In place of the orange zest, switch in one of the following:
• lemon zest, finely grated, 2 teaspoons
• crystallized ginger, finely chopped, 3 tablespoons
• mini chocolate chips, ¼ cup
• pure vanilla extract, 1 teaspoon
• peppermint hard candies, crushed, ¼ cup

In place of the molasses cookies, switch in one of the following:
• soft 3-inch sugar cookies, 16
• soft 3-inch chocolate cookies, 16
• soft 3-inch cinnamon-sugar cookies, 16

Jammin' Sugar Cookie Thumbprints

MAKES 10 COOKIES

granulated sugar
¼ cup + 3 tablespoons

unsalted butter
4 tablespoons, at room
temperature

all-purpose flour
⅔ cup

fruit preserves
¼ cup

1. Heat the oven to 350°F. Line 1 large cookie sheet with a nonstick liner. Put the 3 tablespoons sugar in a small ramekin and set aside.

2. Put the butter and the remaining ¼ cup sugar in a medium bowl. Beat with an electric mixer on low speed until smooth and blended, about 1 minute. Add the flour. Beat on medium-low speed until just blended, about 1 minute.

3. Using your hands, press and roll the dough into 1-inch balls. Roll the balls in the reserved sugar and arrange on the prepared cookie sheet about 1½ inches apart. Using a finger, press down into the middle of each mound to make a well that's almost down to the bottom. (If the edges crack too much, reroll the dough and try again.)

4. Bake until the tops look dry, 12 to 14 minutes. Let the cookies sit for 5 minutes and then transfer them to a rack to cool completely. Serve immediately or cover and store at room temperature for up to 2 days. Just before serving, use a small spoon to drop about ¼ teaspoon of the preserves into the indentation.

Switch-Ins
In place of the fruit preserves, switch in one of the following:
• fruit curd, ¼ cup
• peanut butter, ¼ cup
• Nutella, ¼ cup
• dulce de leche, ¼ cup

In place of the fruit preserves, switch in the following and press into the center wells before baking:
• caramels, 5 small squares, unwrapped, cut in half

Gussy It Up
Top with Chocolate Drizzle (page 178) or Vanilla or Citrus Glaze (page 180).

Toasted Bittersweet "S'more" Bars

MAKES 18 COOKIES

unsalted butter
8 tablespoons, divided

graham cracker crumbs
1 cup

chocolate
(bittersweet or semisweet),
6 ounces, chopped

marshmallows
18 large, cut in half crosswise

1. Heat the oven to 350°F. Line an 8-inch-square baking dish with foil, leaving about 1 inch hanging over 2 edges. Lightly coat the bottom and sides with cooking spray. Make room in the fridge.

2. Put 3 tablespoons of the butter in a medium, heatproof bowl and heat in a microwave until melted. Add the crumbs and stir until well blended. Dump the crumbs into the pan and, using a flat-bottomed cup, firmly press the crumbs into an even layer. Bake until fragrant, about 12 minutes.

3. Put the chocolate and the remaining butter in a medium heatproof bowl and heat in a microwave until melted. Whisk until smooth and blended. Pour into the warm, baked crust and spread evenly. Refrigerate until almost firm, about 30 minutes. Arrange the marshmallow halves, cut side down, evenly over the chocolate, pressing lightly. Cover and refrigerate until very firm, about 40 minutes or for up to 2 days.

4. Just before serving, adjust the oven rack to the top level and heat the broiler on high. Using the excess foil as handles, lift the s'more square from the pan and set on a cookie sheet. Pull the foil away from the sides and slide the cookie sheet under the broiler. Broil until the marshmallows are browned, about 20 seconds. Set on a rack and move the foil and s'more square to a cutting board. Cut into 18 rectangles. Serve immediately or cover and refrigerate for up to 2 days. Serve slightly chilled.

Switch-Ins
In place of the graham cracker crumbs, switch in one of the following:
• gingersnap cookie crumbs, 1 cup
• vanilla wafer cookie crumbs, 1 cup

Gussy It Up
Add the following to the butter-chocolate mixture:
• peanuts, chopped, 2 tablespoons

Lemony Ladyfingers

MAKES 20 COOKIES

large eggs
3, separated and divided

granulated sugar
6 tablespoons, divided

lemon zest
finely grated,
1½ teaspoons

all-purpose flour
½ cup

Tech Talk
If you don't have a pastry bag, fill a heavy-duty zip-top plastic bag with the batter and carefully press out the air without pressing on batter. Zipper-close the bag and snip off a small amount (about ½ inch) of one the bottom corners. Proceed with the piping as directed.

1. Heat the oven to 375°F. Fit a large pastry bag with a plain #7 tip (about ½ inch). Line 2 large cookie sheets with nonstick liners.

2. Put 2 egg yolks (discard the third yolk) in a small bowl and the 3 egg whites in a medium bowl. Beat the whites with an electric mixer on medium speed until foamy. Increase the speed to medium high and beat until the whites hold soft peaks. Continue beating while gradually adding 3 tablespoons of sugar. Beat until medium-firm, glossy peaks form.

3. Add the lemon zest to the yolks. Beat with an electric mixer on medium-high speed until foamy. Gradually add 2 tablespoons of the sugar and beat until pale yellow and thick. When the whisk is lifted, the mixture will fall back into the bowl and form a ribbon.

4. Using a rubber spatula, scoop half of the whites into the yolk mixture. Gently fold until just combined. Sprinkle half of the flour over the mixture and gently fold until just blended. Add the remaining whites and carefully fold in. Sprinkle on remaining flour and gently fold in until just blended.

5. Gently scoop the batter into the pastry bag. Pipe short, thin strips (about 3 inches long and ¾ inch wide) about 1½ inches apart onto the prepared cookie sheets. Sprinkle the remaining sugar over the ladyfingers. Bake until the tops are golden brown, about 13 minutes. Set on a rack and let cool for about 15 minutes. Carefully peel the ladyfingers from the liners. Serve immediately or cover and store at room temperature for up to 2 days.

Switch-Ins
In place of the lemon zest, switch in one of the following:
• pure vanilla extract, 1 teaspoon
• pure almond extract, ½ teaspoon

Chewy Pine Nut–Almond Drops

MAKES 15 COOKIES

almond paste
firmly packed,
⅔ cup (7 ounces),
cut into pieces

confectioners' sugar
1 cup + more for dusting

white from large egg
1

pine nuts
⅔ cup

1. Put the almond paste and confectioners' sugar in a food processor. Process until fine crumbs form, about 30 seconds. Add the egg white and process until well blended and smooth. Refrigerate the dough (still in the bowl) while the oven heats.

2. Heat the oven to 350°F. Line 1 large cookie sheet with a nonstick liner. Put the pine nuts in a small ramekin.

3. Using a mini ice cream scoop, shape the dough into 1-inch balls. Dip the top half of the balls into the pine nuts. Arrange, nut side up, on the prepared cookie sheet about 1 inch apart.

4. Bake until puffed, slightly cracked, and golden brown, 16 to 18 minutes. Let the cookies sit for 5 minutes and then transfer to a rack to cool completely. Just before serving, sift a little confectioners' sugar over the cookies. Serve immediately or cover and store at room temperature for up to 3 days.

Switch-Ins
In place of the pine nuts, switch in one of the following:
• mini chocolate chips, ⅔ cup
• slivered almonds, chopped, ⅔ cup

Gussy It Up
• Mix ½ cup chopped dried apricots into the dough before shaping and baking.
• Coat the cookie tops with Chocolate Drizzle (page 178).

Tech Talk
Almond paste is made with almonds, sugar, and liquid (cane syrup or glycerin). It's available in tubes and cans. I find the tube variety to be the easiest to work with. Don't substitute marzipan for almond paste. While they're essentially the same, marzipan contains more sugar and is more pliable, making it better for shaped candy and confections.

Oatmeal Cinnamon Crisps

MAKES 8 COOKIES

unsalted butter
2 tablespoons, melted

brown sugar
¼ cup, firmly packed

ground cinnamon
¼ teaspoon

**old-fashioned
rolled oats**
⅔ cup

1. Heat the oven to 350°F. Line 1 cookie sheet with a nonstick liner.

2. Put the butter in a small bowl. Add the brown sugar and cinnamon. Stir until well blended. Add the oats. Using a rubber spatula, stir and smear the ingredients together until the oats are moistened and the sugar is evenly dispersed. The mixture will be crumbly.

3. Using a tablespoon measure, scoop up crumbs and press firmly into the measure. Arrange on the prepared cookie sheet about 1½ inches apart. Using a small offset spatula, flatten each mound into a 2-inch round, gently sliding any scattered crumbs back into the round.

4. Bake until the oats are golden brown, 12 minutes. Let the cookies sit for 5 minutes and then transfer them to a rack to cool completely. Serve immediately or cover and store at room temperature for up to 3 days.

Switch-Ins
In place of the ground cinnamon, switch in the following:
• ground ginger, ¼ teaspoon

In place of the old-fashioned rolled oats, switch in the following:
• instant, unflavored oats, ⅔ cup

Gussy It Up
Serve warm cookies with diced ripe pears and Boozy Hard Sauce (page 178) or vanilla ice cream.

Lemon Melt-Aways

MAKES 15 COOKIES

unsalted butter
8 tablespoons, at room temperature

confectioners' sugar
1 cup, divided

lemon zest
finely grated, 1½ teaspoons

all-purpose flour
1 cup

1. Heat the oven to 350°F. Line 1 large cookie sheet with a nonstick liner.

2. Put the butter, ½ cup of the confectioners' sugar, and the lemon zest in a medium bowl. Beat with an electric mixer on low speed until smooth and blended, about 1 minute.

3. Add the flour. Beat on medium-low speed until just blended, about 1 minute.

4. Shape the dough into 1-inch balls. Arrange on the prepared cookie sheet about 2 inches apart.

5. Bake until pale golden brown, about 13 minutes. Set aside to cool slightly. Roll each cookie in the remaining ½ cup confectioners' sugar and set on a rack to cool completely. Serve immediately or cover and store at room temperature for up to 2 days.

Switch-Ins
In place of the lemon zest, switch in one of the following:
• orange zest, finely grated, 1 teaspoon
• ground cinnamon, ¾ teaspoon
• pure vanilla extract, 1 teaspoon

Peppermint Meringue Kisses

MAKES 24 COOKIES

confectioners' sugar
1 cup

whites from large eggs
2

pure peppermint extract
⅛ teaspoon

peppermint hard candies
finely chopped, ⅓ cup

1. Heat the oven to 175°F. Line 1 large cookie sheet with parchment (not a nonstick liner). Sift the confectioners' sugar twice to remove all lumps and divide into two fairly equal portions.

2. Put the egg whites in a medium bowl. Beat with an electric mixer on medium speed until foamy. Increase the speed to medium high and beat until the whites hold soft peaks. Continue beating while gradually adding one portion of confectioners' sugar. Beat until firm, glossy peaks form. Add the peppermint extract and mix briefly. Sift the remaining confectioners' sugar over the meringue and gently fold in until blended.

3. Scoop the meringue into a large pastry bag fitted with a large (#8) star tip. Pipe swirled kisses (about 1½ inches wide and 2 inches high) about 1 inch apart onto the prepared cookie sheet. Sprinkle the finely chopped peppermint candies over the kisses.

4. Bake until dry and crisp, about 3 hours. Turn the oven off and let the meringues cool in the oven for 1 hour. Serve immediately or cover and store at room temperature for up to 1 week.

Switch-Ins
In place of the peppermint extract, switch in the following:
• pure vanilla extract, ¼ teaspoon

In place of the peppermint candies, switch in one of the following:
• pistachios, finely chopped, ⅓ cup
• cinnamon hard candies, finely chopped, ⅓ cup

Gussy It Up
Stir ⅓ cup mini chocolate chips, chopped pistachios, or toasted sweetened shredded coconut into the meringue before shaping and baking.

Change It Up
In place of the pastry bag, drop the meringue by 2 tablespoonfuls on the prepared cookie sheet and continue with the recipe.

Crunchy Peanut Butter Buttons

MAKES 20 COOKIES

crunchy peanut butter
¾ cup

unsalted butter
3 tablespoons, at room temperature

granulated sugar
⅔ cup

large egg
1

1. Heat the oven to 350°F. Line 2 large cookie sheets with nonstick liners.

2. Put the peanut butter, butter, and sugar in a medium bowl. Beat with an electric mixer on low speed until blended, about 1 minute.

3. Add the egg. Beat on medium-low speed until just blended, about 1 minute.

4. Drop the dough 1 tablespoonful at a time on the prepared cookie sheet about 1½ inches apart. Bake until browned around the edges, 12 to 14 minutes. Set on a rack to cool completely. Serve immediately or cover and store at room temperature for up to 3 days.

Switch-Ins
In place of the crunchy peanut butter, switch in the following:
• smooth peanut butter, ¾ cup

Gussy It Up
• Stir ⅓ cup M&M's® Minis® into the batter before shaping and baking.
• Coat some or all of the cookie tops with Chocolate Drizzle (page 178).

Chocolate-Dipped Toasted-Coconut Macaroons

MAKES 10 COOKIES

granulated sugar
¼ cup

white from large egg
1

sweetened shredded coconut
1½ cups, toasted (see page 184 for more info)

chocolate
(bittersweet or semisweet), 2 ounces, melted

1. Heat the oven to 275°F. Line 1 large cookie sheet with parchment.

2. Put the sugar and egg white in a small bowl and whisk until blended and foamy. Add the coconut. Stir until well blended.

3. Mound scant 2 tablespoonfuls of batter onto the prepared cookie sheet about 1½ inches apart. Using slightly dampened fingers, press each mound into a small pyramid. Bake until the cookies are golden brown all over, 20 to 25 minutes. Set on a rack to cool completely.

4. Put the melted chocolate into a small ramekin. Dip the top half of each macaroon into the melted chocolate (you won't need all the chocolate). Arrange, chocolate side up, on a rack and set aside until the chocolate hardens. Serve immediately or cover and store at room temperature for up to 2 days.

Switch-Ins
In place of the bittersweet or semisweet chocolate, switch in one of the following:
• butterscotch chips, ½ cup, melted
• white chocolate, 2 ounces, melted

Gussy It Up
Stir ⅓ cup chopped pistachios or almonds into the batter before shaping and baking.

White Chocolate Haystacks

MAKES 18 COOKIES

gingersnap cookies
coarsely chopped,
2 cups

dried cranberries
¾ cup

dried apricots
coarsely chopped,
½ cup

white chocolate
8 ounces, melted

1. Line 1 large cookie sheet with a nonstick liner and make room in the fridge.

2. Put the chopped cookies, cranberries, and apricots in a medium bowl. Stir until blended. Pour the melted chocolate over the mixture and gently stir and fold until the mixture is evenly coated with the chocolate.

3. Using two large spoons, mound the mixture, 2 tablespoonfuls at a time, onto the prepared sheet about 1 inch apart. Slide the sheet into the fridge and chill until firm, about 30 minutes, or for up to 2 days. Serve slightly chilled or at room temperature.

Switch-Ins
In place of the gingersnaps, switch in one of the following:
• chocolate wafer cookies, chopped, 2 cups
• vanilla wafer cookies, chopped, 2 cups

In place of the dried cranberries, switch in one of the following:
• dried cherries, ¾ cup
• dried figs, coarsely chopped, ¾ cup

Sparkling Ginger Pinwheels

MAKES 20 COOKIES

confectioners' sugar
1 cup, divided

crystallized ginger
finely chopped,
⅓ cup

frozen puff pastry sheet
1 (about 9 ounces), thawed

unsalted butter
2 tablespoons, melted

1. Heat the oven to 400°F. Line 1 large cookie sheet with a nonstick liner.

2. Put ½ cup of the confectioners' sugar and the crystallized ginger in a small bowl. Stir until blended and set aside.

3. Arrange a large piece of plastic wrap on the counter. Using a rolling pin, roll out the puff pastry sheet, sprinkling the top and bottom often and generously with the remaining sugar to prevent sticking, into a 10 x 16-inch rectangle. Pour the melted butter onto the center of the dough and spread evenly with a small offset spatula. Sprinkle the sugar-ginger mixture evenly over the butter.

4. Starting on one short side and using the plastic as a guide, roll up the dough jellyroll style. Pinch the seam to the roll so it sticks together. Wrap the roll and refrigerate until firm, about 45 minutes (for faster chilling, pop the wrapped roll in the freezer).

5. Arrange the roll, seam side down, on a cutting board and cut into ½-inch-thick slices. Arrange the slices on the prepared cookie sheet about 2 inches apart. Bake until golden brown, about 13 minutes. Flip the cookies and continue to cook until golden brown, another 2 to 3 minutes. Set on a rack to cool completely. Serve immediately or cover and store at room temperature for up to 2 days.

Switch-Ins
In place of the crystallized ginger, switch in the following:
• ground cinnamon, 1½ teaspoons

Gussy It Up
Use ⅓ cup of a combination of finely chopped dried fruits like apricots or dates with or without the ginger instead of only crystallized ginger.

Chocolate Toffee Crumble Cups

MAKES 12 COOKIES

unsalted butter
5 tablespoons, at room temperature

confectioners' sugar
½ cup

all-purpose flour
¾ cup

chocolate-covered toffee bars
crushed,
½ cup, divided

1. Heat the oven to 350°F. Line a 12-cup mini muffin pan with paper or foil liners.

2. Put the butter and confectioners' sugar in a medium bowl. Beat with an electric mixer on low speed until blended, about 1 minute. Add the flour and beat on medium-low speed until just blended, about 1 minute. Add ¼ cup of the crushed toffee bits and mix to combine.

3. Shape the dough into 1-inch balls and place in the prepared muffin cups.

4. Bake until the cookies are puffed and pale golden brown and the tops look dry and cracked, 17 to 19 minutes. Set on a rack, sprinkle the remaining toffee bits into the center of each cookie, and let cool completely. Serve immediately or cover and store at room temperature for up to 2 days.

Switch-Ins
In place of the toffee bits, switch in ½ cup of one of the following:
• mini chocolate chips (¼ cup for dough and the remainder for the tops)
• butterscotch chips, chopped (¼ cup for dough and the remainder for the tops)
• peanut butter chips, chopped (¼ cup for dough and the remainder for the tops)

Maple Sugar Tile Cookies

MAKES 10 COOKIES

granulated maple sugar
¼ cup

white from large egg
1

unsalted butter
4 tablespoons, melted

all-purpose flour
¼ cup

1. Heat the oven to 350°F. Line 2 large cookie sheets with nonstick liners. Steady a rolling pin between two bottles or cans so that it's ready to shape the cookies. Arrange a cooling rack next to the pin for the hot cookie sheet.

2. Put the maple sugar and the egg white in a small bowl. Whisk until blended and a bit foamy, about 1 minute. Add the warm (not hot) melted butter and whisk until blended. Add the flour and whisk until smooth.

3. Drop the batter by a scant 1 tablespoon onto the prepared cookie sheets about 4 inches apart (I can fit 5 on a cookie sheet). Spread each round of batter into a 3½-inch circle with a small offset spatula. Bake, one sheet at a time, until the cookies are browned around the edges, 8 to 10 minutes.

4. Working quickly, move the cookie sheet to the cooling rack. Using a wide metal spatula, lift off the hot cookies, one by one, and immediately drape them over the rolling pin. Let cool until set, about 5 minutes. Carefully remove the cookies from the rolling pin and set them on a rack to cool completely. Serve immediately or cover and store at room temperature for up to 3 days.

Switch-Ins
In place of the maple sugar, switch in the following:
• granulated sugar, ¼ cup

Change It Up
In place of the round shape, make swizzle cookies. Cut out a 5 x ½-inch rectangle from the center of a coated paper plate. Lay the stencil on the prepared cookie sheet and thinly spread batter over the opening. Repeat with the remaining batter (no more than 5 per sheet). Bake until golden brown, about 3 to 5 minutes. Working quickly, loosely wrap the hot cookies around the handles of wooden spoons.

Orange-Scented Mini Elephant Ears

MAKES 22 COOKIES

granulated sugar
⅔ cup, divided

orange zest
finely grated,
1 tablespoon

frozen puff pastry sheet
1 (about 9 ounces),
thawed

unsalted butter
2 tablespoons, melted

1. Put ⅓ cup of the sugar and the orange zest in a small bowl. Stir until blended and set aside.

2. Arrange a large piece of plastic wrap on the counter. Using a rolling pin, roll out the puff pastry on the plastic into a 10 x 15-inch rectangle. Sprinkle the top and bottom often and generously with the remaining ⅓ cup sugar to prevent sticking (you won't use it all). Pour the melted butter onto the center of the dough and spread evenly with a small offset spatula. Sprinkle the reserved sugar-orange mixture evenly over the butter.

3. Cut the dough in half crosswise (you'll have two 10 x 7½-inch rectangles). Starting on one short side and using the plastic as a guide, roll up the dough jellyroll style to the center. Roll up the opposite side until the 2 rolls meet in the center. Pinch the rolls so they stick together. Repeat with the remaining dough. Wrap the rolls and refrigerate until firm, about 45 minutes (for faster chilling, pop the wrapped rolls in the freezer).

4. Heat the oven to 425°F. Line 2 large cookie sheets with nonstick liners.

5. Arrange the rolls, seam side down, on a cutting board and cut into ½-inch-thick slices. Arrange on the prepared cookie sheets about 1½ inches apart. Bake until golden brown, about 14 minutes. Turn over and bake for another 1 to 2 minutes until golden brown. Set on a rack to cool completely. Serve immediately or cover and store at room temperature for up to 2 days.

Switch-Ins
In place of the orange zest, switch in the following:
• walnuts, finely chopped, ¼ cup

Gussy It Up
Top with Chocolate Drizzle (page 178).

No-Bake Rocky Road Bundles

MAKES 18 COOKIES

puffed rice cereal
2 cups

mini marshmallows
¾ cup

peanuts
(lightly salted or unsalted),
chopped, ⅓ cup

chocolate
(milk, bittersweet, or
semisweet),
5 ounces, melted

1. Line 1 large cookie sheet with a nonstick liner and make room in the fridge.

2. Put the puffed rice cereal, mini marshmallows, and chopped peanuts in a large bowl. Stir until blended. Pour the melted chocolate over the mixture and gently stir and fold until the mixture is evenly coated with the chocolate.

3. Using two large spoons, mound the mixture, 2 tablespoonfuls at a time, onto the prepared sheet about 1½ inches apart. Slide the sheet into the fridge and chill until firm, about 30 minutes, or for up to 2 days. Serve slightly chilled or at room temperature.

Switch-Ins

In place of the **puffed rice cereal**, switch in the following:
• **corn flakes**, 2 cups

In place of the **peanuts**, switch in one of the following:
• **dried apricots**, chopped, ⅓ cup
• **dried cherries**, ⅓ cup
• **chopped nuts** (hazelnuts, pecans, pistachios, walnuts, almonds, macadamias), ⅓ cup, lightly toasted
• **chocolate chips**, ⅓ cup

Walnut Rugelach

MAKES 17 COOKIES

frozen puff pastry sheet
1 (about 9 ounces), thawed

confectioners' sugar
½ cup

seedless raspberry jam
2 tablespoons

walnuts
finely chopped, ¼ cup

1. Arrange a large piece of plastic wrap on the counter. Using a rolling pin, roll out the puff pastry on the plastic into a 10 x 13-inch rectangle. Sprinkle the top and bottom often and generously with the confectioners' sugar to prevent sticking (you won't use it all). Using an offset spatula, spread the jam evenly over the dough to within ¼ inch of the edges.

2. Cut the dough in half lengthwise (you'll have two 5 x 13-inch rectangles). Starting on one long side and using the plastic as a guide, roll up the dough jellyroll style. Pinch the seam to the roll so it sticks together. Repeat with the remaining dough. Wrap the rolls and refrigerate until firm (for faster chilling, pop the wrapped rolls in the freezer).

3. Heat the oven to 375°F. Line 1 large cookie sheet with nonstick liner.

4. Arrange the rolls, seam side down, on a cutting board and cut into 1½-inch slices. Arrange on the prepared cookie sheet about 1 inch apart. Brush the tops with a little water and sprinkle with the chopped walnuts. Bake until deep golden brown, 23 to 25 minutes. Set on a rack to cool completely. (You can expect some of the jam to leak out.) Serve immediately or cover and store at room temperature.

Switch-Ins
In place of the raspberry jam, switch in one of the following:
• apricot jam, 2 tablespoons
• strawberry jam, 2 tablespoons

In place of the walnuts, switch in the following:
• pistachios, finely chopped, ¼ cup

Some
occasions scream out
for a creamy dessert concoction. Whether
you're celebrating a holiday or birthday or simply in
need of some homey comfort food, turn to this section when
you're dreaming of a velvety rich dessert. ❋ When working with the
recipes here, follow switch-in suggestions closely. While some dairy products
can be swapped, others can't. Half-and-half, for example, will not whip up like
heavy cream. In fact, it won't whip at all. ❋ Unless a switch-in is offered for a pan or

creamy desserts

container, use the exact size called for in the recipe. Unauthorized swaps will affect
baking and/or chilling time. ❋ When working with gelatin desserts, be sure to
soften and dissolve the gelatin properly and chill until set, using the time as a
guide and not the rule depending on your fridge's temperature. To double-
check yours, place a refrigerator thermometer in the center of your
fridge and check the temp after 24 hours. It should be 38°F.
If not, you may be able to adjust your dials up or down
to correct the temp.

Spiced Mango Whip

SERVES 4

mangos
medium, ripe,
2 (14 ounces each), halved
and pitted (see page 183)

brown sugar
1/3 cup, firmly packed

ground cinnamon
1/4 teaspoon

heavy cream
1 cup

1. Have ready 4 serving bowls or cups and make room in the fridge.

2. Cut the flesh of each mango half into 1-inch crosshatch without piercing the skin. Push up from the skin side (it will look like a porcupine) and cut away the mango from the skin.

3. Pile the mango into a food processor and add the brown sugar and cinnamon. Process until smooth, about 1 minute. Taste and add more sugar or cinnamon, if needed.

4. Put the heavy cream in a medium bowl. Beat with an electric mixer until firm peaks form when the beaters are lifted (don't forget to stop the mixer before lifting!).

5. Add about two-thirds of the purée to the whipped cream. Using a rubber spatula, gently fold in until well blended. Add the remaining purée and fold in just until some mango purée streaks are still visible. Spoon the mixture into the bowls. Cover and refrigerate until ready to serve or for up to 2 days.

Switch-Ins
In place of the brown sugar, switch in the following:
• granulated sugar, 1/3 cup

In place of the cinnamon, switch in one or more of the following:
• fresh mint leaves, finely chopped, 1 tablespoon
• lime zest, finely grated, 1 teaspoon
• fresh ginger, finely grated, 1 teaspoon
• orange zest, finely grated, 1 teaspoon

Gussy It Up
• Serve in fun glass stemware or parfait glasses for a festive look.
• It's a parfait! Layer the whip with fresh fruit (small mango chunks, kiwis, berries). You can even layer in crushed crisp cookies (gingersnaps, chocolate wafers, amaretti).

Café au Lait Cheesecake

SERVES 6 TO 8

**instant coffee
granules**
1 tablespoon

cream cheese
three 8-ounce packages,
at room temperature

brown sugar
1⅓ cups, firmly packed

large eggs
3

1. Heat the oven to 325°F. Lightly grease an 8 x 2-inch round cake pan. Have ready 1 shallow baking pan that will hold the cake pan.

2. Dissolve the coffee granules in 1 tablespoon water in a small ramekin. Put the cream cheese in a medium bowl. Beat with an electric mixer on medium speed until very smooth, about 3 minutes.

3. Add the brown sugar and the dissolved coffee. Beat on medium-low speed until well blended, about 1 minute.

4. Add the eggs, one at a time, mixing until just incorporated. Scrape the batter into the prepared pan and set inside the baking pan. Fill the baking pan with enough hot water to come halfway up the sides of the cake pan.

5. Bake until the center of the cheesecake barely jiggles when nudged, about 55 minutes. Set the baking pan on a rack to cool completely. Remove the cake pan from the water. Tap the edge of the cake pan on the counter to loosen the cheesecake. Position a flat plate over the pan and invert. Lift the pan off the cake and place a flat serving plate on the cake and invert again. Cover and refrigerate until ready to serve or for up to 3 days (or freeze for up to 1 month). Serve chilled.

Switch-Ins
In place of the coffee granules, switch in one or more of the following:
• pure vanilla extract, 1½ teaspoons
• orange zest, finely grated, 1 tablespoon

In place of the brown sugar, switch in the following:
• granulated sugar, 1⅓ cups

Gussy It Up
Serve with a drizzle of Killer Chocolate Sauce (page 179) or a dollop of one of the whipped creams (page 180).

Individual Rich Cocoa Puddings

SERVES 4

granulated sugar
¾ cup

unsweetened cocoa powder
(preferably Dutch processed), ½ cup

cornstarch
⅓ cup

whole or 2% milk
3 cups, divided

1. Have ready four 6-ounce ramekins and make room in the fridge.

2. Put the sugar, cocoa powder, and cornstarch in a medium saucepan and whisk until blended. Add about ½ cup of the milk and whisk until a smooth paste forms. Whisk in the remaining milk.

3. Cook, whisking frequently, over medium heat until boiling. Boil, whisking constantly, for 1 minute.

4. Pour the pudding into the ramekins. Cover with plastic wrap (touching the surface so that a skin doesn't form). Serve warm or refrigerate until ready to serve or for up to 2 days.

Switch-Ins
In place of the granulated sugar, switch in the following:
• brown sugar, ¾ cup, firmly packed

In place of the milk, switch in the following:
• half-and-half, 3 cups

Gussy It Up
• Serve with Classic Sweetened Whipped Cream (page 180) and/or chocolate shavings.
• Add 1½ teaspoons finely grated orange zest along with the sugar.
• Add ½ teaspoon ground cinnamon along with the sugar.

Mini Bittersweet Chocolate Cheesecakes

SERVES 6

cream cheese
one 8-ounce package, at
room temperature

granulated sugar
⅓ cup

chocolate
(bittersweet or
semisweet),
4 ounces, chopped,
divided, and melted

large egg
1

1. Heat the oven to 300°F. Line 6 standard muffin tins with foil liners and lightly grease with cooking spray.

2. Put the cream cheese in a medium bowl. Beat with an electric mixer on medium speed until very smooth, about 2 minutes.

3. Add the sugar and 3 ounces of melted chocolate. Beat on medium-low speed until well blended, about 1 minute. Add the egg and mix until just incorporated.

4. Spoon the batter into the muffin cups. Bake until the centers of the cheesecakes barely jiggle when nudged, 15 to 18 minutes. Set the muffin tin on a rack to cool completely. Cover and refrigerate until ready to serve or for up to 3 days (or freeze for up to 1 month). Just before serving, drizzle with the remaining 1 ounce melted chocolate (rewarmed, if needed).

Switch-Ins
In place of the granulated sugar, switch in the following:
• brown sugar, ⅓ cup, firmly packed

In place of the bittersweet or semisweet chocolate, switch in the following:
• white chocolate, 5 ounces, divided, melted (use 4 ounces in the cheesecake mixture and 1 ounce for drizzling)

Gussy It Up
• Add 1 teaspoon finely grated orange zest along with the cream cheese.
• Add ½ teaspoon instant coffee granules dissolved in 1 teaspoon vanilla extract along with the cream cheese.
• Serve with a few fresh raspberries and a drizzle of Killer Chocolate Sauce (page 179) or Classic Sweetened Whipped Cream (page 180).

Maple Cornmeal "Indian" Puddings

SERVES 4

whole or 2% milk
2 cups

pure maple syrup
½ cup + more for drizzling

cornmeal
finely ground,
4 tablespoons

yolks
from large eggs
2

1. Have ready four 6-ounce ramekins or small serving bowls and make room in the fridge.

2. Put all the ingredients in a medium saucepan and whisk until blended. Cook, whisking frequently, over medium heat until boiling. Boil, whisking constantly, for 3 minutes.

3. Pour the pudding into the ramekins or bowls. Cover with plastic wrap (touching the surface so that a skin doesn't form). Serve warm or refrigerate until ready to serve or for up to 3 days. If you like, drizzle each pudding with a little maple syrup just before serving.

Switch-Ins
In place of the milk, switch in the following:
• half-and-half, 2 cups

In place of the maple syrup, switch in the following:
• brown sugar, ½ cup, firmly packed

Gussy It Up
• Add 2 teaspoons finely grated orange zest.
• Add ¼ teaspoon ground cinnamon and a pinch of ground nutmeg.
• Serve with Classic Sweetened Whipped Cream (page 180).
• Serve with fresh fruit, like sliced bananas or apricots.

No-Bake Chocolate Pots

SERVES 4

heavy cream
1 cup

chocolate
(bittersweet or
semisweet),
6 ounces, chopped

unsalted butter
4 tablespoons, cut up

pure vanilla extract
1 teaspoon

1. Have ready four 6-ounce ramekins and make room in the fridge.

2. Heat the heavy cream in a medium saucepan or in the microwave in a medium bowl until just boiling. Add the chocolate, butter, and vanilla. Whisk until smooth and blended.

3. Pour the mixture into the ramekins. Cover with plastic wrap (not touching the chocolate). Refrigerate until chilled (for faster chilling, pop them in the freezer) and thickened or for up to 3 days.

Switch-Ins
In place of the vanilla, switch in one or more of the following:
- orange zest, finely grated, 1 teaspoon
- ground cinnamon, ¼ teaspoon
- dark rum or brandy, 1 tablespoon
- instant coffee granules, 1 teaspoon
- unsweetened cocoa powder, 1 tablespoon

Gussy It Up
- Because these "pots" don't see any oven time, be creative with the vessels. Using small crystal wineglasses or even small espresso cups, called demitasse, will really dress up this rich dessert.
- Top the "pots" with one or all of these garnishes: a dollop of Classic Sweetened Whipped Cream (page 180), a few fresh raspberries, and/or shaved chocolate.

Coconut Crème Caramel

SERVES 4

coconut milk
1 can (13 to 14 ounces)

granulated sugar
⅔ cup, divided

large eggs
3 whole + 1 yolk

ground cardamom
¼ teaspoon

1. Heat the oven to 325°F. Have ready four 6-ounce ramekins and 1 shallow baking pan that will hold the ramekins (I use a 9-inch round cake pan). Make room in the fridge.

2. Pour the coconut milk into a medium saucepan. Bring to a boil over medium-high heat and cook until reduced to 1½ cups, about 8 minutes.

3. Meanwhile, put ⅓ cup of the sugar and 1 tablespoon water in a small saucepan. Cook over low heat until the sugar is dissolved and the mixture is boiling. Increase the heat to medium and boil, without stirring, until the sugar is medium-amber, 2 to 3 minutes. Gently swirl the pan to even out the caramel color. Pour the hot caramel evenly into the ramekins. Swirl each ramekin to cover the bottom with caramel. Arrange in the baking pan and set aside.

4. Put the remaining ⅓ cup sugar, the eggs, yolk, and cardamom in a medium bowl and whisk until blended. Slowly add the hot coconut milk, whisking constantly, until blended. Pour the mixture into the ramekins. Fill the baking pan with enough hot water to come halfway up the sides of the ramekins.

5. Bake until the custards jiggle when nudged, about 40 minutes. Transfer the pan to a rack to cool the custards completely. Cover and refrigerate until cold, at least 6 hours or for up to 2 days. To serve, run a small knife between the custards and the ramekins (see page 184 for more info). Quickly invert each onto a serving plate and shake gently to loosen the custard.

Switch-Ins
In place of the cardamom, switch in one of the following:
• pure vanilla extract, ½ teaspoon
• lemon zest, finely grated, ½ teaspoon

Gussy It Up
Serve with toasted coconut.

Classic Vanilla Bean Pot de Crèmes

SERVES 4

heavy cream
2 cups

vanilla bean
½ bean, split

granulated sugar
⅓ cup

**yolks
from large eggs**
4

1. Heat the oven to 325°F. Arrange four 6-ounce ramekins in a shallow baking pan (I use a 9-inch round cake pan). Make room in the fridge.

2. Put the heavy cream and vanilla bean in a medium saucepan. Cook over medium-high heat until boiling. Slide the pan from the heat, cover, and set aside for 15 minutes for the vanilla bean to infuse the cream. Fish out the bean pod and, using a small knife, scrape the seeds into the cream.

3. Put the sugar and yolks in a medium bowl and whisk until blended. Return the cream to a simmer then slowly add to the yolks, whisking constantly, until blended. Skim the foam from the top and pour the mixture into the ramekins. Fill the baking pan with enough hot water to come halfway up the sides of the ramekins.

4. Bake until the custards jiggle when nudged, 30 to 34 minutes. Carefully transfer the ramekins to a rack, covering loosely with foil, to cool completely. Cover and refrigerate until cold, at least 6 hours or for up to 2 days.

Switch-Ins
In place of the heavy cream, switch in the following:
• half-and-half, 2 cups

In place of the vanilla bean, switch in one of the following:
• pure vanilla extract, ¾ teaspoon (add to the yolk–sugar mixture)
• fresh ginger, finely grated, 1 teaspoon (add to the heavy cream before heating)

Gussy It Up
Serve with chocolate shavings or a few fresh berries or Chocolate Whipped Cream (page 180).

Butterscotch Risotto Pudding

SERVES 4

whole or 2% milk
4 cups

arborio rice
⅔ cup

brown sugar
½ cup, firmly packed

pure vanilla extract
1 teaspoon

1. Have ready four serving bowls and make room in the fridge.

2. Put the milk and rice in a large saucepan. Bring to a boil over medium-high heat. Reduce the heat to low and simmer, stirring, until the rice is tender and the pudding is thick and reduced to about 3 cups, 25 to 30 minutes. Stir more frequently toward the end of cooking to prevent scorching.

3. Slide the pan from the heat and stir in the brown sugar and vanilla. Pour the pudding into the serving bowls. Cover with plastic wrap (touching the surface so that a skin doesn't form). Serve warm or refrigerate until ready to serve or for up to 2 days. If the pudding is too thick, stir in a little more milk.

Switch-Ins
In place of the milk, switch in the following:
• half-and-half, 4 cups

In place of the brown sugar, switch in the following:
• granulated sugar, ⅓ cup

Gussy It Up
Just before serving, sprinkle with chopped chocolate-covered toffee candy bars or chopped toasted pecans, hazelnuts, or walnuts.

Blueberry Yogurt Panna Cotta

SERVES 4

gelatin
unflavored powdered,
2 teaspoons

blueberries
2 pints (12 ounces each),
rinsed and dried, divided

granulated sugar
⅓ cup

plain yogurt
(preferably Greek style)
½ cup

1. Have ready four 6-ounce ramekins and make room in the fridge.

2. Pour 3 tablespoons water into a small cup or ramekin and sprinkle the gelatin on top. Let sit until the gelatin is moist and plump, about 3 minutes.

3. Pile 1½ pints of the blueberries, the sugar, and 3 tablespoons water into a medium saucepan. Cook, stirring, over medium-low heat until the sugar is dissolved and the fruit is soft and juicy, about 3 minutes. Pour into a food processor or blender and process until smooth, about 30 seconds. Taste and add more sugar, if needed.

4. Strain the mixture through a fine-mesh sieve into a medium mixing bowl, pressing on the solids (you'll have about 2¼ cups). Discard the remaining solids. Add the gelatin to the hot blueberry mixture and stir until well blended. Set aside to cool slightly, about 5 minutes. Whisk in the yogurt until blended. Skim the foam from the top and pour the mixture into the ramekins. Cover and refrigerate until ready to serve or for up to 3 days.

5. To serve, run a small knife between the custards and the ramekins and dip the bottoms into hot water (see page 184 for more info). Quickly invert each onto a serving plate and shake gently to loosen the panna cotta. Serve with remaining fresh blueberries sprinkled on top.

Switch-Ins
In place of the blueberries, switch in the following:
• raspberries, 2 pints (12 ounces each)

Orange "Creamsicle" Rice Pudding

SERVES 4

navel orange
large, 1

whole or 2% milk
3½ cups

long- or medium-grain white rice
½ cup

granulated sugar
⅓ cup

1. Have ready a medium bowl and make room in the fridge.

2. Finely grate 2 teaspoons zest from the orange and set aside. Cut away all the zest and pith (see page 184) from the orange then cut the orange crosswise into ¼-inch slices. Cover and refrigerate the slices until ready to serve.

3. Put the milk and rice in a large saucepan. Bring to a boil over high heat. Reduce the heat to low, cover, and simmer, stirring occasionally for 15 minutes. Uncover and continue to simmer, stirring, until the rice is tender and the pudding is reduced to about 3 cups, about 10 minutes. Stir more frequently toward the end of cooking to prevent scorching.

4. Slide the pan from the heat and stir in the sugar and orange zest. Pour the pudding into a medium bowl and cover with plastic wrap (touching the surface so that a skin doesn't form). Refrigerate until chilled or for up to 3 days. Serve the pudding in bowls with sliced oranges.

Switch-Ins
In place of the orange zest, switch in the following:
• pure vanilla extract, 1 teaspoon (add with the sugar)

In place of the milk, switch in the following:
• half-and-half, 3½ cups

Gussy It Up
Just before serving, top with toasted coconut or a few orange sections, raspberries, or cut-up strawberries.

Vanilla Coeur à la Crème with Strawberries

SERVES 4

cream cheese
4 ounces, at room temperature

vanilla yogurt
16 ounces

confectioners' sugar
1 cup, divided

strawberries
1 quart (1 pound), rinsed, dried, and hulled

1. Line 4 small coeur à la crème molds with two layers of cheesecloth, with enough of the ends hanging over the sides to cover the tops. Set the molds on a small jellyroll pan (to hold the drained liquid) and make room in the fridge.

2. Put the cream cheese in a medium bowl. Beat with an electric mixer until smooth, about 2 minutes. Add the yogurt and 1/2 cup of the confectioners' sugar and beat until well blended.

3. Pour the mixture into the lined molds, mounding slightly. Fold the cheesecloth ends over the tops. Refrigerate overnight or for up to 1 day before serving.

4. To make the sauce, set aside 2 strawberries for garnish. Pile the remaining strawberries and remaining 1/2 cup confectioners' sugar into a food processor or blender and process until smooth. Taste and add more confectioners' sugar, if needed. Cover and refrigerate for up to 4 days.

5. To serve, unwrap the coeurs à la crème and invert onto small serving plates. Cut the reserved strawberries in half lengthwise and arrange one on top of each heart. Spoon the sauce around the base and serve immediately.

Switch-Ins
In place of the vanilla yogurt, switch in one of the following:
• strawberry, peach, or blueberry yogurt, 16 ounces

Change It Up
You can use 1 large coeur à la crème mold in place of the 4 small ones. Or, you can line a large wire-meshed sieve with cheesecloth, set it in a medium bowl, and proceed with the recipe. Invert the finished crème onto a large plate and scoop servings onto dessert plates.

Strawberry Shortcake Trifle

SERVES 4 TO 6

strawberries
1 quart (1 pound), rinsed, dried, and hulled; divided

heavy cream
1 cup

confectioners' sugar
½ to ¾ cup (depending on the berries' sweetness)

crisp vanilla wafer cookies
40 to 50 (depending on the shape of the bowl)

Tech Talk
The 6-cup, round Glad® plastic storage container with lid is perfect for taking this trifle on the road.

1. Have ready a small 6-cup glass or trifle bowl and make room in the fridge.

2. Pile half of the strawberries into a food processor or blender. Process until smooth, about 1 minute (you'll have about 1 cup). Thinly slice the remaining strawberries and divide into 3 piles.

3. Pour the heavy cream and ½ cup of the confectioners' sugar into a medium bowl. Beat with an electric mixer until firm peaks form when the beaters are lifted (don't forget to stop the mixer before lifting!). Pour the strawberry purée into the whipped cream. Using a rubber spatula, gently fold until well blended. Taste and add more confectioners' sugar, if desired.

4. Spoon about 1 cup of the strawberry cream into the glass bowl. Arrange a single layer of cookies, slightly overlapping, on top of the cream, pressing lightly on each one. Scatter one pile of sliced strawberries on top of the cookies. Repeat layering with the remaining cream, cookies, and strawberries, ending with a layer of cream and decoratively arranging the remaining sliced berries. You'll have a total of 3 layers of cream, 2 layers of cookies (not including the garnish), and 2 layers of strawberries, not including the garnish. Cover and refrigerate for at least 8 hours or for up to 1 day. Just before serving, arrange a few of the remaining cookies and the strawberries on top of the cream. Serve chilled.

Switch-Ins
In place of the vanilla wafer cookies, switch in the following:
• crisp chocolate wafer cookies, 20 to 30 (depending on the shape of the bowl)

Gussy It Up
Serve with a drizzle of Killer Chocolate Sauce (page 179) or a sprinkling of chopped fresh mint.

Whipped Caramel Toffee Ice Box Trifle

SERVES 4 TO 6

heavy cream
1¾ cups, divided

granulated sugar
½ cup

**chocolate-covered
toffee candy bits**
½ cup

chocolate cookies
crisp and thin,
20 to 30 (depending on
the shape of the bowl)

Tech Talk
The 6-cup, round
Glad plastic storage
container with lid is
perfect for taking
this dessert on
the road.

1. Have ready a 6-cup glass or trifle bowl and make room in the fridge.

2. Put ³/₄ cup of the cream in a small saucepan or microwave-safe bowl and heat until very warm. Set aside. Put the sugar and 2 tablespoons water in a small saucepan. Cook over low heat until the sugar is dissolved and the mixture is boiling. Increase the heat to medium and boil, without stirring, until the sugar is medium amber, 2 to 3 minutes. Gently swirl the pan to even out the caramel color. Slide the pan from heat and add the warm cream. (Be careful—the steam is very hot.) Whisk until completely smooth. If necessary, return the pan to the heat and continue whisking until the caramel is dissolved. Refrigerate until chilled, about 1 hour.

3. Pour the remaining 1 cup heavy cream into a medium bowl and add the chilled caramel. Beat with an electric mixer until medium-firm peaks form when the beaters are lifted (don't forget to stop the mixer before lifting!). Fold in half of the crushed toffee bar pieces until blended.

4. Spoon about ¹/₃ cup of the caramel cream into the serving bowl. Arrange a single layer of cookies, slightly overlapping, on top of the cream, pressing lightly on each one. Spread about ¹/₃ cup of the cream over the cookies. Repeat layering with the remaining cookies and cream, ending with a layer of cream. You'll have a total of 5 layers of cream and 4 layers of cookies. Sprinkle the remaining toffee bits over the top. Cover and refrigerate for at least 8 hours or for up to 2 days. Serve chilled.

Switch-Ins

In place of the chocolate-covered toffee bits, switch in the following:
• chopped pecans, ½ cup, toasted

In place of the chocolate cookies, switch in the following:
• vanilla wafer cookies, 40 to 50 (depending on the shape of the bowl)

Meyer Lemon–Ricotta Panna Cotta

SERVES 4

Meyer lemons
3

gelatin
unflavored powdered,
2 teaspoons

ricotta
(part skim or whole),
1⅓ cups

granulated sugar
½ cup

1. Have ready four 6-ounce ramekins and make room in the fridge.

2. Finely grate the zest of 1 lemon or enough to measure 2 teaspoons. Squeeze all the lemons and strain the liquid to measure ⅔ cup.

3. Put ⅓ cup of the lemon juice in a small bowl or ramekin and sprinkle the gelatin on top. Let sit until the gelatin is moist and plump, about 3 minutes. Microwave until the gelatin is dissolved and the liquid is clear, 30 to 90 seconds.

4. Pile the ricotta, granulated sugar, zest, and remaining ⅓ cup lemon juice in a blender. Cover and process until smooth and blended, about 1 minute. Taste and add more sugar, if needed. Add the dissolved gelatin and process until blended, about 20 seconds.

5. Pour the mixture into the ramekins. Cover the ramekins with plastic wrap, not touching the custard, and refrigerate until chilled and firm, about 2 hours, or for up to 3 days.

6. To serve, run a small knife between the custards and the ramekins and dip the bottoms into hot water (see page 184 for more info). Quickly invert each onto a serving plate and shake gently to loosen the panna cotta.

Switch-Ins
In place of the Meyer lemon juice and zest, switch in the following:
• lemon zest, finely grated, 1½ teaspoons
• fresh lemon juice, ⅔ cup

Dark Chocolate–Banana Soufflés

SERVES 6

granulated sugar
⅓ cup, divided + more for dusting

chocolate
(bittersweet or semisweet),
3 ounces, chopped

banana
medium, very ripe
1 (4½ ounces), peeled

large eggs
3 whites + 1 yolk

1. Heat the oven to 400°F. Lightly grease six 6-ounce ramekins with cooking spray and sprinkle granulated sugar in the ramekins, tilting to coat completely. Tip out the excess and arrange on a small jellyroll pan.

2. Put the chocolate in a medium heatproof bowl and melt in the microwave or over simmering water. Set aside to cool until barely warm, about 5 minutes. Add half of the sugar, the banana, egg yolk, and 1 tablespoon water. Whisk until smooth and blended.

3. Put the egg whites in a medium bowl. Beat with an electric mixer until soft peaks form when the beaters are lifted. Continue beating while gradually adding the remaining sugar. Beat until medium-firm peaks form. Whisk about a quarter of the whites into the chocolate–banana mixture until blended. Add the remaining whites and, using a rubber spatula, gently fold in until just blended.

4. Spoon the mixture into the prepared ramekins. Bake until the soufflés are puffed and jiggle when nudged, about 13 minutes. Serve immediately.

Make Ahead
Put the filled, uncooked ramekins in the freezer until firm. Cover with plastic wrap and freeze for up to 1 month. To bake, heat the oven to 400°F. When the oven is hot, remove the soufflés from the freezer, unwrap, and arrange on a small jellyroll pan. Bake until the soufflés are puffed and jiggle when nudged, about 16 minutes.

Switch-Ins
In place of the granulated sugar, switch in the following:
• confectioners' sugar, ½ cup, divided + more for dusting

Gussy It Up
Serve with a dollop of Classic Sweetened Whipped Cream (page 180).

In place of the water, add the following:
• dark rum or brandy 1 tablespoon

Tech Talk
Bananas with lots of dark brown-black peel have the best flavor and are easiest to mash up. If you don't have a banana on your counter like this, put it in a zip-top bag and seal for 24 to 36 hours to ripen quickly. Very ripe bananas can be frozen for future use.

Orange-Scented White Chocolate–Blackberry Mousse

SERVES 4

heavy cream
1⅓ cups, divided

white chocolate
4 ounces, chopped

orange-flavored liqueur
1 tablespoon

blackberries
1 pint (12 ounces), rinsed and dried

1. Have ready 4 small serving bowls or wineglasses and make room in the fridge.

2. Put ⅓ cup of the cream and the chocolate in a large heatproof bowl and heat in the microwave or over simmering water until the chocolate is melted. Whisk until smooth and blended. Refrigerate until chilled. (For faster cooling, put the bowl over an ice-filled bowl and stir gently until chilled.)

3. Add the remaining 1 cup cream to the white chocolate mixture. Beat with an electric mixer until medium-firm peaks form when the beaters are lifted. Add the liqueur and mix briefly.

4. Set aside a few blackberries for garnish. Add the remaining blackberries to the white chocolate mixture and, using a rubber spatula, gently fold in until just blended. Spoon the mixture into the serving bowls or glasses. Cover and refrigerate until ready to serve or for up to 2 days. Serve chilled, with the remaining blackberries on top.

Switch-Ins
In place of the orange-flavored liqueur, switch in one of the following:
• orange zest, finely grated, 1 teaspoon
• almond-flavored liqueur, 1 tablespoon
• hazelnut-flavored liqueur, 1 tablespoon

In place of the blackberries, switch in one of the following:
• raspberries, 1 pint
• blueberries, 1 pint
• amaretti cookies, crushed, 1½ cups
• hazelnuts, chopped, 1 cup, toasted

Gussy It Up
Instead of folding in the berries, layer the cream and berries parfait-style and garnish with the reserved berries and a mint sprig or two.

Fresh Fig–Lemon Cream Gratin

SERVES 4

heavy cream
¼ cup

lemon curd
½ cup

figs
large, firm-ripe,
12 (9 ounces total),
trimmed

pound cake
four 1-inch slices, lightly
toasted

1. Heat the oven to 425°F. Have ready a shallow 4-cup gratin dish or pie plate.

2. Put the heavy cream and lemon curd in a small bowl and whisk until smooth and well blended. Scrape into the prepared gratin dish and spread evenly.

3. Cut the figs in half lengthwise. Arrange, cut side up, in a single layer in the lemon cream.

4. Bake until the figs are juicy and the lemon cream is bubbling around the edges, 9 to 12 minutes. Serve hot or warm over toasted pound cake slices.

Switch-Ins
In place of the figs, switch in the following:
• medium, ripe apricots, 6, quartered
• strawberries, 1½ pints, rinsed, dried, and cut in half
• cherries, 9 ounces, rinsed, dried, and pitted

For the lemon curd, switch in:
• orange curd, ½ cup

For the pound cake, switch in one of the following:
• angel food cake, four 2-inch slices
• soft ladyfingers, 8, split

Gussy It Up
Serve with a dollop of Classic Sweetened Whipped Cream (page 180).

In place of the water, add the following:
• dark rum or brandy, 1 tablespoon

Stir 1 tablespoon orange- or lemon-flavored liqueur into the cream-curd mixture.

Sprinkle the finished dessert with chopped, toasted hazelnuts or pistachios.

Crushed Raspberry–Mascarpone Whip

SERVES 4

raspberries
1½ pints (18 ounces),
rinsed and dried

granulated sugar
½ cup, divided

mascarpone
8 ounces

heavy cream
¾ cup

1. Have ready 4 small serving bowls or wineglasses and make room in the fridge.

2. Set aside about 12 raspberries for garnish. Put the remaining berries and ¼ cup of the sugar in a medium bowl and lightly crush with a rubber spatula. Set aside.

3. Put the mascarpone, heavy cream, and remaining ¼ cup sugar in a medium bowl. Beat with an electric mixer until medium-firm peaks form when the beaters are lifted (don't forget to stop the mixer before lifting!).

4. Spoon about 3 tablespoons of the cream into the serving bowls or glasses. Top with about ¼ cup of the crushed berries. Spread about 3 tablespoons cream over the berries. Repeat layering with the remaining berries and cream. You'll have a total of 3 layers of cream and 2 layers of raspberries not including the garnish. Cover and refrigerate until ready to serve or for up to 1 day. Serve chilled with the remaining whole raspberries on top.

Switch-Ins
In place of the raspberries, switch in one of the following:
• blackberries, 1½ pints (18 ounces)
• blueberries, 1½ pints (18 ounces)
• medium, ripe peaches, 3, pitted and chopped

Gussy It Up
Fold 1 tablespoon finely chopped lemon basil into the whipped cream before layering it with the fruit. Garnish with the reserved berries and small sprigs of lemon basil.

Dulce de Leche "Bread Pudding" Gratin

SERVES 6

pound cake
1 (10¾-ounce) loaf,
thawed if frozen

heavy cream
⅔ cup

dulce de leche
½ cup

banana
large, ripe, 1, peeled
and thinly sliced

1. Arrange an oven rack about 4 inches from the broiler and heat the broiler on high. Arrange 6 shallow gratin dishes on a jellyroll pan. Cut the pound cake into ¾-inch cubes and measure out 4 cups (nibble on the remainder or save and add to your next batch of homemade ice cream).

2. Put the heavy cream in a medium bowl. Beat with an electric mixer until medium-firm peaks form when the beaters are lifted (don't forget to stop the mixer before lifting!). Add the dulce de leche and mix briefly.

3. Add the pound cake cubes and the sliced bananas to the whipped cream and, using a rubber spatula, gently fold them in. Divide among the prepared dishes and spread evenly.

4. Broil, rotating the pan, until the tops are browned, 2 to 3 minutes. Serve immediately.

Switch-Ins
In place of the pound cake, switch in the following:
• angel food cake

In place of the banana, switch in the following:
• ripe mango, 1, cut into small chunks

Gussy It Up
After removing the gratin dishes from the oven, sprinkle the tops with mini chocolate chips or chopped hazelnuts.

Chocolate Decadence for a Crowd

SERVES 10

chocolate
(bittersweet or
semisweet),
10 ounces,
chopped

unsalted butter
10 tablespoons

**confectioners'
sugar**
1 cup, divided

large eggs
4

1. Heat the oven to 300°F. Lightly grease an 8 x 2-inch round cake pan and line the bottom with a nonstick liner.

2. Put the chocolate and butter in a medium heatproof bowl and heat in a microwave or over simmering water until melted. Whisk until smooth and blended. Set aside to cool slightly.

3. Put ²/₃ cup of the confectioners' sugar and the eggs in a medium bowl. Beat with an electric mixer on medium-high speed until very thick, about 3 minutes. Turn the mixer to low, gradually pour in the chocolate mixture, and continue beating until well blended. Pour the batter into the prepared pan and spread evenly.

4. Bake until the top is slightly puffed and a pick comes out with gooey crumbs, about 40 minutes. Set on a rack to cool for 1¹/₂ hours. Run a knife between the cake and the inside of the pan. Invert onto a flat plate, then remove the pan and liner. Invert again onto a flat serving plate; cool completely. Cover and refrigerate until chilled or for up to 2 days. To serve, sift the remaining confectioners' sugar over the top and cut into wedges.

Switch-Ins
In place of the ²/₃ cup confectioners' sugar in the cake, switch in the following:
• granulated sugar, ¹/₂ cup
• brown sugar, ¹/₂ cup, firmly packed

Gussy It Up
Add one of the following to the butter–chocolate mixture:
• dark rum or orange-flavored liqueur, 1¹/₂ tablespoons
• instant espresso powder, 1 teaspoon dissolved in 1¹/₂ teaspoons of pure vanilla extract

Serve with a drizzle of Double Whole Berry Sauce (page 178), Espresso or Vanilla-Reduced Cream Sauce (page 179), or fresh fruit.

Key Lime–Peach Trifle

SERVES 6

cream cheese
8 ounces,
at room temperature

**sweetened
condensed milk**
1 can (14 ounces)

Key lime juice
bottled, or fresh,
⅔ cup

peaches
ripe, white and/or orange,
5, rinsed and dried

1. Have ready a small 6-cup glass or trifle bowl and make room in the fridge.

2. Put the cream cheese in a medium bowl. Beat with an electric mixer until smooth, about 2 minutes. Add the condensed milk and Key lime juice and beat until well blended. Set aside.

3. Cut the peaches in half and remove the pit. Thinly slice one half and set aside for garnish. Coarsely chop the remaining peach halves (you should have about 4½ to 5 cups).

4. Spoon about 1½ cups fruit into the glass bowl. Spread about a third of the Key lime cream over the fruit. Repeat layering with the remaining fruit and cream, ending with a layer of cream. You'll have a total of 3 layers of peaches and 3 layers of cream, not including the garnish. Cover and refrigerate for at least 30 minutes or for up to 4 hours. The cream will thicken as it chills. Garnish with the reserved sliced peaches and serve chilled.

Switch-Ins
In place of the Key lime juice, switch in the following:
• fresh lemon juice, ⅔ cup

In place of the peaches, switch in the following:
• assorted sliced fresh fruit or berries, 5 cups

Gussy It Up
Sprinkle ¼ cup crushed cookie crumbs (chocolate or gingersnap) over the first two layers of cream.

Tech Talk
The 6-cup, round Glad plastic storage container with lid is perfect for taking this dessert on the road.

Sweet Cherry Amaretti Parfaits

SERVES 4

cherries
¾ pound, rinsed, dried, and pitted

granulated sugar
½ cup, divided

heavy cream
1¼ cups

amaretti cookies
crushed,
1½ cups

1. Have ready 4 small serving bowls or wineglasses and make room in the fridge.

2. Set aside about 8 whole cherries for garnish. Roughly chop the remaining cherries and put in a medium bowl with ¼ cup of the sugar. Lightly toss with a rubber spatula. Set aside.

3. Put the heavy cream and the remaining ¼ cup sugar in a medium bowl. Beat with an electric mixer until medium-firm peaks form when the beaters are lifted (don't forget to stop the mixer before lifting!).

4. Spoon about 2 tablespoons of the cookie crumbs into the serving bowls or glasses. Spoon about 2 tablespoons of the cream over the crumbs. Top with about ¼ cup of the cherries. Repeat layering with the remaining cookie crumbs, cream, and cherries, ending with cream. You'll have a total of 3 layers of cookie crumbs, 3 layers of cream, and 2 layers of cherries, not including the garnish. Cover and refrigerate until ready to serve or for up to 1 day. Serve chilled, with the remaining whole cherries on top.

Switch-Ins
In place of the cherries, switch in one of the following:
• blackberries, 1½ pints
• blueberries, 1½ pints

In place of the amaretti cookies, switch in one of the following:
• gingersnap cookie crumbs, 1½ cups
• cinnamon cookie crumbs, 1½ cups
• chocolate cookie crumbs, 1½ cups

Gussy It Up
Add 1 tablespoon dark rum or orange-flavored liqueur to the cherry–sugar mixture or top with Chocolate Drizzle (page 178).

Spiked Eggnog Custard

SERVES 4

gelatin
unflavored powdered,
2 teaspoons

eggnog
1⅔ cups

dark rum
2 to 3 tablespoons

ground nutmeg
¼ teaspoon

1. Have ready four 6-ounce ramekins and make room in the fridge.

2. Put ¼ cup water in a small bowl or ramekin and sprinkle the gelatin on top. Let sit until the gelatin is moist and plump, about 3 minutes. Microwave until the gelatin is dissolved and the liquid is smooth, 30 to 90 seconds.

3. Put the eggnog and dark rum in a medium bowl. Add the dissolved gelatin and whisk until blended, about 20 seconds.

4. Pour the mixture into the ramekins. Cover and refrigerate until chilled and firm or for up to 3 days.

5. To serve, sprinkle the nutmeg evenly over the top of each custard and serve immediately.

Switch-Ins
In place of the dark rum, switch in one of the following:
• brandy, 2 to 3 tablespoons
• pure vanilla extract, 1 teaspoon

Gussy It Up
Serve with one of the caramel sauces (page 179), Ruby Red Cranberry Sauce (page 179), or Killer Chocolate Sauce (page 179).

Change It Up
This custard can be inverted and served like a panna cotta. Run a small knife between the custards and the ramekins and dip the bottoms into hot water (see page 184 for more info). Quickly invert onto a plate and shake gently to loosen the custard. Sprinkle with nutmeg and serve.

Kiwi Lemon Mousse

SERVES 4

heavy cream
1 cup

lemon curd
⅔ cup

kiwis
medium, ripe,
2, peeled and
coarsely chopped

soft ladyfingers
6 whole, separated

1. Have ready 4 serving bowls or glasses and make room in the fridge. Set aside about ¼ cup chopped kiwi for garnish.

2. Put the heavy cream in a medium bowl. Beat with an electric mixer until firm peaks form when the beaters are lifted (don't forget to stop the mixer before lifting!).

3. Add about two-thirds of the lemon curd into the whipped cream. Using a rubber spatula, gently fold in until well blended. Add the remaining curd and fold in just until some yellow streaks are still visible.

4. Arrange 3 ladyfingers, rounded side facing out, around the inside of each bowl or glass. Spoon about 3 tablespoons of the cream into the serving bowls or glasses. Top with about 2 tablespoons of the chopped kiwi. Spoon about 3 tablespoons cream over the kiwis. Repeat layering with the remaining kiwi and cream. You'll have a total of 3 layers of cream and 2 layers of kiwi, not including the garnish. Cover and refrigerate until ready to serve or for up to 1 day. Serve chilled, with the remaining kiwi on top.

Switch-Ins
In place of the lemon curd, switch in one of the following:
• orange curd, ⅔ cup
• grapefruit curd, ⅔ cup

In place of the ladyfingers, switch in the following:
• pound cake, 12 slices (2 inches long and about ½ inch thick)

Gussy It Up
• This whip is no-bake so use fun glass stemware or parfait glasses for a festive look.
• Just before serving, drizzle with a little Easy Butterscotch Sauce (pages 178–179) or one of the caramel sauces (page 179).

Creamy Espresso Pudding for Two

SERVES 2

brown sugar
¼ cup, firmly packed

cornstarch
1 tablespoon

instant espresso powder
1¾ teaspoons

half-and-half
1¼ cups, divided

1. Have ready two 6-ounce ramekins and make room in the fridge.

2. Put the brown sugar, cornstarch, and instant espresso powder in a small saucepan and whisk until blended. Add about ¼ cup of the half-and-half and whisk until the coffee is almost dissolved. Whisk in the remaining half-and-half.

3. Cook, whisking frequently, over medium heat until boiling. Boil, whisking constantly, for 1 minute.

4. Pour the pudding into the ramekins. Cover with plastic wrap (touching the surface so that a skin doesn't form). Serve warm or refrigerate until ready to serve or for up to 1 day.

Switch-Ins
In place of the brown sugar, switch in the following:
• granulated sugar, ¼ cup

In place of the instant espresso powder, switch in the following:
• instant coffee granules, 1¾ teaspoons

In place of the half-and-half, switch in the following:
• whole milk, 1¼ cups, divided

Gussy It Up
• Just before serving, top with chocolate-covered espresso beans or chocolate shavings.
• Serve with Classic Sweetened Whipped Cream (page 180) or Chocolate Whipped Cream (page 180).

Pistachio Lemon Soufflés

SERVES 4

granulated sugar
2 tablespoons + more for
the ramekins

lemon curd
⅓ cup

pistachios
medium-finely chopped,
3 tablespoons

**whites from large
eggs**
3

1. Heat the oven to 400°F. Lightly grease four 6-ounce ramekins with cooking spray and sprinkle granulated sugar in the ramekins, tilting to coat completely. Gently tip out the excess and arrange the ramekins on a small jellyroll pan.

2. Put the lemon curd and 1 tablespoon water in a medium bowl and whisk until smooth and blended. Stir in the pistachios.

3. Put the egg whites in a medium bowl. Beat with an electric mixer until soft peaks form when the beaters are lifted (don't forget to stop the mixer before lifting!). Continue beating while gradually adding the sugar. Beat until medium-firm peaks form. Whisk about a quarter of the whites into the lemon mixture until blended. Add the remaining whites and, using a rubber spatula, gently fold in until just blended.

4. Spoon the mixture into the prepared ramekins. Bake until the soufflés are puffed and the tops are brown, about 14 minutes. Serve immediately.

Switch-Ins
In place of the lemon curd, switch in the following:
• orange curd, ⅓ cup

In place of the pistachios, switch in the following:
• toasted hazelnuts, medium-finely chopped, 3 tablespoons
• toasted pecans, medium-finely chopped, 3 tablespoons

Gussy It Up
In place of the water, add one of the following:
• lemon-flavored liqueur, 1 tablespoon
• orange-flavored liqueur, 1 tablespoon

This
section embraces all
things frozen, from frozen yogurts and
granitas to ice pops and flavor-packed sundaes and ice
cream sandwiches. Regardless of your skill level and time con-
straint, there's a frosty, icy, creamy snack or dessert waiting for you. To
guarantee your frozen desserts firm up and stay frozen, place a freezer thermometer in the middle of your freezer. After about 24 hours, check the temperature. The optimum temp is zero. If it's warmer or colder than that, adjust the freezer's

frozen desserts

temp according to the manufacturer's instructions. ❋ Keep your desserts in top-quality
taste, texture, and shape by wrapping them tightly and storing them away from the
door. Cover containers with lids and/or double layers of plastic wrap to keep other
flavors and odors from sneaking into your frozen treats. ❋ If you've made your
frozen sherbet, sorbet, ice cream, granita, or pie ahead of time, unless
otherwise directed, let it sit on the counter for 5 to 10 minutes to soften
slightly to make scooping and serving easier.

Pink Lemonade Ice Pops

MAKES 4 ICE POPS

granulated sugar
½ cup

strawberries
4, rinsed, dried, hulled,
and quartered

lemon zest
2 strips

fresh lemon juice
½ cup

1. Have ready four 5- to 6-ounce ice pop molds and make room in the freezer, making sure the molds are level and secure.

2. Put the sugar, strawberries, lemon zest strips, and ½ cup water in a small saucepan. Bring to a boil over medium-high heat. Reduce the heat and simmer, stirring occasionally, until the berries are very soft, about 3 minutes. Set aside to cool completely or, for faster cooling, set the pan over a bowl filled with ice and stir gently until chilled.

3. Set a fine-mesh sieve over a large bowl or 4-cup measure. Pour the cooled strawberry syrup into the sieve and, using a rubber spatula, press on the berries; discard the seeds and fibrous pulp. Strain the liquid again without pressing on the solids to remove any remaining seeds.

4. Add the lemon juice and ⅔ cup cold water to the mixture and stir until well blended, making pink lemonade. Divide the pink lemonade among the molds. Cover each mold with foil and push a wooden ice pop stick through it and into the middle of each pop. Freeze until firm, about 2 hours, or for up to 3 days. To serve, remove the foil and slip the ice pops from the molds.

Switch-Ins
In place of the lemon zest, switch in the following:
• lime zest, 2 strips

In place of the lemon juice, switch in the following:
• fresh lime juice, ½ cup

Gussy It Up
Add a small sprig of fresh lemon thyme or rosemary to the pan along with the sugar, strawberries, and water. Remove before straining.

Change It Up
In place of the ice pop molds, pour the pink lemonade into four 5-ounce paper cups. Cover each cup with foil and freeze until firm.

Marbled Chocolate Peppermint Ice Cream Sandwiches

MAKES 8 ICE CREAM SANDWICHES

chocolate ice cream
1 pint

French vanilla ice cream
1 pint

chocolate cookies
soft 3 inch,
16

peppermint hard candies
crushed,
1½ cups

1. Position a small cookie sheet in the freezer so that it lays flat.

2. Scoop both flavors of ice cream into a medium bowl. Using a large spoon, mash them together until marbled but not completely combined. If the ice cream is super soft, pop the bowl into the freezer for a few minutes to firm up.

3. Arrange 8 cookies, flat side up, on the counter. Using a ¼-cup ice cream scoop, divide the semi-firm ice cream mixture evenly onto the cookies. Top with the remaining cookies, flat side down. Press slightly to spread the ice cream to the edges. Arrange on the cookie sheet set in the freezer. Chill until firm, about 1 hour.

4. Put the crushed candies in a small bowl. Working with one sandwich at a time, roll the outside edge in the candies, pressing with your fingers. Return the sandwiches to the freezer until ready to serve. The sandwiches can be served immediately or wrapped in plastic and stored in the freezer for up to 1 month.

Switch-Ins
In place of the chocolate and French vanilla ice creams, switch in any flavors you like.

In place of the crushed peppermint candies, switch in one of the following:
• mini chocolate chips, 1½ cups
• chopped nuts, 1½ cups, toasted
• colored sprinkles, 1½ cups
• toffee bits, 1½ cups
• sweetened shredded coconut, 1½ cups, toasted (see page 184 for more info)

Triple Chocolate–Raspberry Ice Cream Pie

SERVES 6 TO 8

**chocolate cookie
pie crust**
1 (6 ounces)

chocolate ice cream
2 pints

raspberries
1½ pints (18 ounces),
rinsed and dried, divided

**chocolate fudge
sauce**
⅔ cup

1. Make room in the freezer for the pie crust.

2. Remove the ice cream from the freezer and let soften at room temperature until it's just barely spreadable. Scoop the ice cream into a medium bowl. Add about half of the raspberries and gently stir until almost blended. Using a rubber spatula, spread the ice cream evenly into the prepared crust. Cover with plastic wrap. Place the pie in the freezer and freeze until hard, about 6 hours or for up to 3 days, before serving.

3. To serve, unwrap the ice cream pie. Spread the fudge sauce evenly over the ice cream and scatter the remaining raspberries on top. Cut the frozen pie into wedges using a sharp knife dipped in hot water.

Switch-Ins

In place of the chocolate cookie pie crust, switch in one of the following:
• graham cracker pie crust, 1 (6 ounces)
• shortbread cookie pie crust, 1 (6 ounces)
• gingersnap cookie pie crust, 1 (6 ounces)

In place of the chocolate ice cream, switch in any flavor you like.

In place of the raspberries, switch in one of the following:
• blackberries, 1½ pints
• blueberries, 1½ pints

In place of the fudge sauce, switch in one of the following:
• slivered almonds, 1 cup, toasted
• macadamia nuts, coarsely chopped, 1 cup, toasted
• pistachios, coarsely chopped, 1 cup, toasted

Mocha Rocky Road Pie

SERVES 6 TO 8

large marshmallows
24

**mocha fudge swirl
ice cream**
2 pints

**chocolate cookie
pie crust**
1 (6 ounces)

pecan halves
½ cup, toasted

1. Make room in the freezer for the pie crust. Using scissors, cut the marshmallows in half at sharp angles. Set aside.

2. Remove the ice cream from the freezer and let soften at room temperature until it's just barely spreadable. Using a large spade or large serving spoon, scoop the ice cream into the chocolate cookie pie crust. Using a rubber spatula, spread the ice cream in an even layer, mounding it slightly in the center.

3. Arrange the cut marshmallows and toasted pecan halves over the top of the ice cream, pressing them lightly into the ice cream. Make sure the marshmallow tips are pointing in many directions. Cover with plastic wrap. Return the pie to the freezer and freeze until hard, about 6 hours or for up to 3 days.

4. To serve, unwrap the pie. Cut the frozen pie into wedges using a sharp knife dipped in hot water. By the time the pie is sliced, the marshmallows will be soft enough to eat.

Switch-Ins
In place of the mocha fudge ice cream, switch in any flavor you like.

In place of the chocolate cookie pie crust, switch in one of the following:
• graham cracker pie crust, 1 (6 ounces)
• shortbread cookie pie crust, 1 (6 ounces)
• gingersnap cookie pie crust, 1 (6 ounces)

In place of the pecans, switch in one of the following:
• walnut halves, ½ cup, toasted
• macadamia nuts, chopped, ½ cup, toasted

Gussy It Up
Serve with Chocolate Whipped Cream (page 180) and Chocolate Drizzle (page 178).

Frozen Chocolate-Covered Banana Nuggets

SERVES 4 TO 6

chocolate
(bittersweet or
semisweet),
8 ounces, chopped

unsalted butter
5 tablespoons

ripe bananas
4

pistachios
chopped,
⅓ cup

1. Line a small cookie or baking sheet or a large flat plate with foil and make room in the freezer.

2. Put the chocolate and butter in a small heatproof bowl and heat in a microwave or over simmering water until melted. Whisk until smooth and blended.

3. Peel the bananas and cut into 1-inch slices. Using a fork, position one banana slice on top of the tines. Lower into the warm chocolate-butter mixture until completely covered. Lift up, tap the fork gently on the edge of the bowl to remove excess chocolate, and arrange on the prepared sheet or plate. Dip the remaining banana slices, one at a time, arranging them about 1 inch apart on the sheet. Sprinkle the chopped pistachios over the chocolate-coated nuggets.

4. Arrange the sheet in the freezer. Chill until very firm, about 1 hour. Lift the nuggets from the foil, pop into a heavy-duty freezer bag or container, and keep frozen until ready to serve, for up to 1 month.

Switch-Ins

In place of the bananas, switch in one of the following:
• ripe mangos, 2, cut into 1-inch pieces
• ripe papayas, 2, cut into 1-inch pieces

In place of the pistachios, switch in one of the following:
• macadamia nuts, chopped, ⅓ cup, toasted
• walnuts, chopped, ⅓ cup, toasted
• colored sprinkles, ¼ cup
• sweetened shredded coconut, ¼ cup

Raspberry Mango Sorbet Pie

SERVES 6 TO 8

shortbread cookie pie crust
1 (6 ounces)

raspberry sorbet
2 pints, divided

mango sorbet
1 pint

pistachios
chopped,
⅔ cup

1. Make room in the freezer for the pie crust.

2. Remove 1 pint of raspberry sorbet from the freezer and let soften at room temperature until it's just barely spreadable. Using a large spade or large serving spoon, scoop the sorbet into the pie crust. Using a rubber spatula, spread the sorbet in an even layer. Arrange the pie crust in the freezer and chill until firm, about 30 minutes.

3. Remove the remaining sorbets from the freezer and let soften at room temperature until they're just barely spreadable. Remove the pie crust from the freezer. Using a small, round ice cream scoop, scoop alternate flavors of sorbets and snugly arrange in the pie crust on top of the raspberry layer. Sprinkle the chopped pistachios over the top. Cover with plastic wrap. Return the pie to the freezer and freeze until hard, about 2 hours or for up to 3 days, before serving.

4. To serve, unwrap the pie. Cut the frozen pie into wedges using a sharp knife dipped in hot water.

Switch-Ins
In place of the shortbread cookie pie crust, switch in one of the following:
• graham cracker pie crust, 1 (6 ounces)
• chocolate cookie pie crust, 1 (6 ounces)
• gingersnap cookie pie crust, 1 (6 ounces)

In place of the raspberry and mango sorbets, switch in any flavors you like.

In place of the pistachios, switch in one of the following:
• colored sprinkles, ⅓ cup
• toffee bits, ½ cup
• crystallized ginger, finely chopped, ¼ cup

Gussy It Up
Serve with Classic Sweetened Whipped Cream (page 180), one of the caramel sauces (page 179), or Killer Chocolate Sauce (page 179).

Roasted Double Strawberry
Ice Cream Sundaes

SERVES 4

strawberries
1 quart (1 pound), rinsed, dried, and hulled

granulated sugar
⅓ cup

**strawberry
ice cream**
1½ pints

**chocolate cookie
crumbs**
½ cup

1. Heat the oven to 450°F. Have ready an 8-inch-square baking dish and four parfait glasses or wineglasses.

2. If the strawberries are very large, cut them in half. Put the berries in the baking dish and add the sugar. Toss until combined and spread in a single layer. Bake, stirring twice, until the strawberries are juicy and tender, about 15 minutes. Set aside to cool slightly or cover and refrigerate until ready to serve or for up to 2 days.

3. To serve, reheat the strawberries until warm, if necessary. Line up the parfait or wineglasses. Beginning and ending with the prepared strawberries and juices, layer the strawberries, ice cream, and cookie crumbs into the glasses. You'll have a total of 3 layers of strawberries, 2 layers of cookie crumbs, and 2 layers of ice cream. Serve immediately.

Switch-Ins
In place of the strawberry ice cream, switch in any flavor you like.

In place of the chocolate cookie crumbs, switch in one of the following:
• graham cracker crumbs, ½ cup
• shortbread cookie crumbs, ½ cup
• gingersnap cookie crumbs, ½ cup

Gussy It Up
Serve with a dollop of Classic Sweetened Whipped Cream (page 180), Killer Chocolate Sauce (page 179), and a chocolate-covered strawberry or a mint sprig.

Grown-Up Creamy Key Lime–Honey Pops

MAKES 6 ICE POPS

Key lime juice
(fresh or bottled),
½ cup

honey
⅔ cup

half-and-half
1⅓ cups

lemon-flavored vodka
1 tablespoon

1. Have ready six 5- to 6-ounce ice pop molds and make room in the freezer, making sure the molds are level and secure.

2. Put the Key lime juice and honey in a bowl. Whisk until well blended. Slowly add the half-and-half, whisking constantly, until blended. Whisk in the flavored vodka.

3. Pour an equal amount of the Key lime mixture into the molds. Cover each mold with foil and push a wooden ice pop stick through the foil and into the middle of each pop. Freeze until firm, about 2 hours, or for up to 3 days.

4. To serve, remove the foil and slip the ice pops from the molds.

Switch-Ins
In place of the Key lime juice, switch in one of the following:
• fresh lemon juice, ½ cup
• fresh lime juice, ½ cup

In place of the lemon vodka, switch in one of the following:
• unflavored vodka, 1 tablespoon
• half-and-half, 1 tablespoon

Change It Up
In place of the ice pop molds, pour the Key lime mixture into six 5-ounce paper cups. Cover each cup with foil and freeze until firm.

Creamy Cran-Raspberry Sherbet

SERVES 4 TO 6

cran-raspberry juice cocktail
2 cups

cranberries
(fresh or frozen),
2 cups

granulated sugar
1 cup

heavy cream
1⅓ cups

1. Have ready an ice cream maker.

2. Put the juice, cranberries, and sugar in a medium saucepan. Cook, stirring, over medium heat until boiling. Reduce the heat to medium low and simmer, stirring occasionally, until the berries have popped, about 6 minutes.

3. Strain the mixture through a fine-mesh sieve into a large bowl, pressing firmly on the solids (discard the solids). Set the liquid aside to cool completely, then refrigerate until chilled or for up to 1 day. For faster cooling, set the bowl over a bowl filled with ice and stir occasionally until well chilled.

4. Arrange an 8-inch-square pan in the freezer, making sure it's level and secure. Add the heavy cream to the berry mixture and whisk until blended. Pour the chilled mixture into the ice cream maker and process according to the manufacturer's instructions. Serve immediately (it will be soft) or scrape into the chilled pan, cover, and freeze until firm or for up to 2 days.

Switch-Ins
In place of the cran-raspberry juice, switch in the following:
• cranberry juice cocktail, 2 cups

In place of the heavy cream, switch in one of the following:
• water, 1⅓ cups
• half-and-half, 1⅓ cups

Gussy It Up
• Mix ½ cup mini chocolate chips or chopped chocolate into the just-churned sherbet.
• Serve with Killer Chocolate Sauce (page 179).
• Serve in chocolate-coated or plain waffle cups.
• Add 1 tablespoon finely grated orange zest to the cranberry mixture.

Frozen Mexican Hot Chocolate Pops

MAKES 4 ICE POPS

half-and-half
1½ cups, divided

Mexican chocolate
4 ounces, chopped

granulated sugar
3 tablespoons

coffee-flavored liqueur
1 tablespoon

1. Have ready four 5- to 6-ounce ice pop molds and make room in the freezer, making sure the molds are level and secure.

2. Put ½ cup of the half-and-half, the chopped chocolate, and the sugar in a small heatproof bowl and heat in a microwave or over simmering water until melted. Whisk until smooth with no gritty bits left undissolved. Reheat if necessary. Add the remaining half-and-half and the coffee liqueur and whisk until blended. To keep the chocolate mixture from separating during freezing, refrigerate, stirring occasionally, until it's cold or, for faster chilling, set the bowl over a bowl filled with ice and stir frequently until cold.

3. Pour an equal amount of the chocolate mixture into the molds. Cover each mold with foil and push a wooden ice pop stick through the foil and into the middle of each pop. Freeze until firm, about 2 hours, or for up to 3 days.

4. To serve, remove the foil and slip the ice pops from the molds.

Switch-Ins
In place of the Mexican chocolate, switch in all of the following:
- semisweet chocolate, 4 ounces, chopped
- granulated sugar, 2 tablespoons (in addition to what's called for)
- ground cinnamon, ¼ teaspoon

In place of the coffee-flavored liqueur, switch in one of the following:
- dark rum, 1 tablespoon
- orange-flavored liqueur, 1 tablespoon
- fresh orange juice, 1 tablespoon
- half-and-half, 1 tablespoon

Change It Up
In place of the ice pop molds, pour the chocolate mixture into six 5-ounce paper cups. Cover each cup with foil and freeze until firm.

Ginger–Meyer Lemon Sherbet

SERVES 4 TO 6

Meyer lemons
4

granulated sugar
1½ cups

heavy cream
½ cup

crystallized ginger
finely chopped,
2 tablespoons

1. Have ready an ice cream maker. Finely grate the zest of 1 lemon or enough to measure 2 teaspoons. Squeeze all the lemons and strain the liquid to measure ⅔ cup.

2. Put the juice, zest, and sugar in a medium saucepan. Cook, stirring, over medium heat until the sugar is dissolved, about 3 minutes. Slide the pan from the heat and add 1½ cups cold water and the heavy cream. Stir until blended. Don't worry if it looks curdled. Refrigerate until chilled or for up to 1 day. For faster cooling, set the bowl over a bowl filled with ice and stir occasionally until well chilled.

3. Arrange a 4½ x 8¼-inch loaf pan in the freezer, making sure it's level and secure. Pour the chilled mixture into the ice cream maker and process according to the manufacturer's instructions. Just before the sherbet is firm, add the ginger into the just-churned ice cream. Serve immediately (it will be soft) or scrape into the chilled loaf pan, cover, and freeze until firm or for up to 2 days.

Switch-Ins
In place of the Meyer lemons, switch in the following:
• lemons, 4

In place of the heavy cream, switch in the following:
• milk, ½ cup

In place of the crystallized ginger, switch in the following:
• fresh mint, finely chopped, 1 tablespoon

Gussy It Up
Serve with a drizzle of one of the caramel sauces (page 179), Double Whole Berry Sauce (page 178), Ruby Red Cranberry Sauce (page 179), or crisp ginger or chocolate cookies.

Fresh Ginger–Plum Granita

SERVES 4 TO 6

plums
ripe, 4 (1¼ pounds),
rinsed, dried, halved, and
pitted

granulated sugar
¾ cup

fresh ginger
finely grated,
2 to 3 teaspoons

pure vanilla extract
¼ teaspoon

1. Arrange a 9 x 13-inch baking dish in the freezer, making sure it's level and secure. Thinly slice 1 plum half; cover and refrigerate until serving. Coarsely chop the remaining plums.

2. Put the chopped plums, sugar, ginger, and 1 cup water in a medium saucepan. Cook, stirring, over medium-high heat until boiling. Reduce the heat to medium low and simmer, stirring, until the plums are very soft, 7 to 10 minutes. Spoon the plums and some of the liquid into a food processor or blender and process until smooth, about 30 seconds.

3. Strain the mixture and the remaining juices through a fine-mesh sieve into a medium bowl, pressing on the solids; discard the solids. Add 1 cup water and the vanilla. Let cool completely, then refrigerate until chilled or for up to 1 day. For faster cooling, set the bowl over a bowl filled with ice and stir occasionally until well chilled.

4. Pour the chilled mixture into the baking dish and freeze for about 2 hours. After that, every 30 minutes, stir, smash, and scrape the mixture with a table fork until the ice crystals are loose and frozen. Serve with the sliced plums on top.

Switch-Ins
In place of the plums, switch in the following:
• ripe apricots, 1 pound

In place of the fresh ginger, switch in the following:
• lemon zest, finely grated, 2 teaspoons

Change It Up
To make a sorbet, follow the directions for making the mixture. Pour the chilled mixture into an ice cream maker (instead of the baking dish) and process according to the manufacturer's instructions. Serve immediately (it will be soft) or scrape into a chilled dish, cover, and freeze until firm or for up to 2 days.

Mixed Berry Granita for Two

SERVES 2

mixed berries
frozen unsweetened,
1 package (12 ounces)

**cran-raspberry
juice cocktail**
½ cup

granulated sugar
⅓ cup

fresh lemon juice
1 tablespoon

1. Arrange a 4-cup dish in the freezer, making sure it's level and secure.

2. Pile the frozen berries, juice, sugar, and lemon juice into a food processor. Pulse briefly until combined. Process until smooth, about 1 minute.

3. Serve immediately (it will be soft) or scrape into the chilled dish, cover, and freeze until firm enough to scoop, about 1 hour, or for up to 2 days.

Switch-Ins
In place of the frozen unsweetened mixed berries, switch in one of the following:
• frozen blueberries, 1 package (12 ounces)
• frozen strawberries, 1 package (12 ounces)

In place of the cran-raspberry juice cocktail, switch in one of the following:
• fresh orange juice, ½ cup
• half-and-half, ½ cup

Gussy It Up
Serve with Killer Chocolate Sauce (page 179) or top with fresh fruit.

Spicy Orange Mango Sorbet

SERVES 4 TO 6

navel orange
large, 1

granulated sugar
¾ cup

mangos
ripe, 2 (about ¾ pound
each), halved

jalapeño
finely chopped,
½ to 1½ teaspoons
(depending on heat level)

1. Have ready 1 or 2 ice cube trays and make room in the freezer. Finely grate the zest of the orange or enough to measure 2 teaspoons. Squeeze the orange and strain the liquid to measure ¾ cup.

2. Put the juice, zest, and sugar in a small saucepan. Cook, stirring, over medium heat until the sugar is dissolved, about 3 minutes. Set aside to cool completely or refrigerate for up to 1 day. For faster cooling, set the bowl over a bowl filled with ice and stir occasionally until well chilled.

3. Cut the flesh of each mango half into 1-inch crosshatch without piercing the skin. Push up from the skin side (it will look like a porcupine) and cut away the mango from the skin. Pile the mango into a food processor and add the orange juice mixture and the jalapeño. Process until smooth, about 1 minute. Taste and add more jalapeño, if needed.

4. Pour into the ice cube trays and freeze until hard, about 4 hours. Pop the frozen mango cubes out of the trays and put them in a heavy-duty zip-top freezer bag. To serve, put the cubes (as many as you'd like) in the food processor. Process until smooth, about 30 seconds. Spoon into serving bowls and serve immediately.

Switch-Ins
In place of the jalapeño, switch in one of the following:
• ground cayenne, pinch
• fresh basil, finely chopped, 1 tablespoon
• pure vanilla extract, ½ teaspoon

Gussy It Up
Serve with crisp ginger or spice cookies.

Tech Talk
To test a jalapeño's heat level, slice off the stem end and quickly touch the inside to the tip of your tongue. If you get a zing, then start with the lower amount of jalapeño in the recipe and add more to taste.

Creamy Mocha Semifreddo

SERVES 4 TO 6

chocolate
(bittersweet or
semisweet),
6 ounces, chopped

granulated sugar
½ cup

**instant coffee
granules**
1½ teaspoons

heavy cream
⅓ cup

1. Have ready 2 ice cube trays and make room in the freezer.

2. Put the chocolate, sugar, instant coffee granules, and 2 cups water in a medium saucepan. Cook, stirring, over medium-low heat until the chocolate is melted and the sugar is dissolved, about 3 minutes. Add the heavy cream and whisk until blended. Set aside to cool completely or refrigerate for up to 1 day. For faster cooling, set the pan over a bowl filled with ice and stir occasionally until well chilled.

3. Pour into the ice cube trays and freeze until hard, about 4 hours. Pop the frozen mocha cubes out of the trays and put into a heavy-duty zip-top freezer bag.

4. To serve, put up to 14 cubes (enough for 2 servings) in a food processor. Process until smooth, about 30 seconds. Repeat as needed with the remaining cubes. Spoon into serving bowls and serve immediately.

Switch-Ins
In place of the instant coffee granules, switch in one of the following:
- pure vanilla extract, ¾ teaspoon
- orange zest, finely grated, 1 teaspoon
- liqueur (orange, coffee, or raspberry flavored), 1 tablespoon

In place of the heavy cream, switch in the following:
- milk, ⅓ cup

Gussy It Up
Top with a dollop of Classic Sweetened Whipped Cream (page 180), a couple of fresh raspberries or some orange zest, and a drizzle of Killer Chocolate Sauce (page 179).

Toasted Almond–Cherry Frozen Yogurt

SERVES 4

pitted cherries
frozen unsweetened,
1 package (12 ounces)

plain yogurt
(preferably Greek style),
1¼ cups

granulated sugar
¾ cup

slivered almonds
chopped,
½ cup, toasted

1. Arrange a 4½ x 8¼-inch loaf pan in the freezer, making sure it's level and secure.

2. Pile the frozen cherries, yogurt, and sugar into a food processor. Process until smooth, about 1 minute. Taste and add more sugar, if needed. Add the almonds and process briefly.

3. Scrape into the chilled dish, cover, and freeze until firm enough to scoop, about 1 hour, or for up to 2 days.

Switch-Ins

In place of the cherries, switch in one of the following:
- frozen mango chunks, 1 package (12 ounces)
- frozen blueberries, 1 package (12 ounces)
- frozen strawberries, 1 package (12 ounces)

In place of the toasted almonds, switch in one of the following:
- mini chocolate chips, ½ cup
- white chocolate, 4 ounces, finely chopped

Gussy It Up

Serve with chocolate shavings or chopped, toasted nuts.

Minty Melon Sorbet

SERVES 4 TO 6

granulated sugar
1 cup

melon
small, ripe,
1 (4 pounds)

fresh mint
finely chopped,
2 tablespoons

fresh lime juice
1 tablespoon

1. Have ready an ice cream maker. Put the sugar and 1 cup water in a medium saucepan. Cook, stirring, over medium heat until the sugar is dissolved, about 3 minutes. Set aside to cool completely or refrigerate for up to 1 day. For faster cooling, set the bowl over a bowl filled with ice and stir occasionally until well chilled.

2. Cut the melon in half, scoop out the seeds, and cut the flesh into 1- to 2-inch chunks. Pile the melon into a food processor and process until smooth, about 1 minute. Add $2^{1}/_{2}$ cups of the fruit purée to the sugar syrup along with the mint and lime juice, and stir until blended. Set aside to cool completely, then refrigerate until chilled or for up to 1 day. For faster cooling, set the bowl over a bowl filled with ice and stir occasionally until well chilled.

3. Arrange a $4^{1}/_{2}$ x $8^{1}/_{4}$-inch loaf pan in the freezer, making sure it's level and secure. Pour the chilled mixture into the ice cream maker and process according to the manufacturer's instructions. Serve immediately (it will be soft) or scrape into the chilled loaf pan, cover, and freeze until firm or for up to 2 days.

Switch-Ins
In place of the mint, switch in the following:
• dried lavender, chopped, 1 teaspoon

In place of the lime juice, switch in the following:
• fresh lemon juice, 1 tablespoon

Change It Up
To make a granita, arrange a 9 x 13-inch baking dish or 9½-cup rectangular plastic container (Ziploc®) in the freezer, making sure it's level and secure. Follow the directions for making the mixture. Pour the chilled mixture into the baking dish and freeze for about 2 hours. After that, every 30 minutes, stir, smash, and scrape the mixture with a table fork until the ice crystals are loose and frozen.

Just Peachy Ice Cream

SERVES 4 TO 6

peaches
ripe, 4 (1 pound), rinsed
and dried

granulated sugar
½ cup

half-and-half
2 cups

pure vanilla extract
1¼ teaspoons

1. Have ready an ice cream maker. Arrange a 4½ x 8¼-inch loaf pan in the freezer, making sure it's level and secure.

2. Cut the peaches in half and discard the pits. Coarsely chop the flesh and pile into a food processor, along with the sugar. Process until smooth, about 1 minute. Taste and add more sugar, if needed. Add the half-and-half and vanilla and process briefly.

3. Pour the peach mixture into the ice cream maker and process according to the manufacturer's instructions. Serve immediately (it will be soft) or scrape into the chilled dish, cover, and freeze until firm, about 1 hour, or for up to 2 days.

Switch-Ins
In place of the vanilla extract, switch in one of the following and add to the just-churned ice cream:
- mini chocolate chips, ½ cup
- crisp cookies (Oreo®, gingersnap, coconut), crumbled, ½ cup
- peach schnapps, 1 tablespoon

Gussy It Up
Garnish with fresh diced peaches or strawberries and gingersnap or vanilla wafer cookie crumbs or granola.

Mix one of the following into the just-churned ice cream:
- chocolate-covered espresso beans, crushed, ⅓ cup
- Nutella, ⅓ cup
- crushed cookies, ⅔ cup (any flavor)
- nuts (any type), chopped, ½ cup, toasted
- crystallized ginger, chopped, ⅓ cup
- chips (white, bittersweet, semisweet, or milk chocolate; butterscotch or peanut), coarsely chopped, ½ cup
- chocolate-covered toffee bars, chopped, ½ cup

Serve with Double Whole Berry Sauce (page 178), one of the caramel sauces (page 179), or Killer Chocolate Sauce (page 179).

Classic Vanilla Ice Cream

SERVES 4 TO 6

half-and-half
2¾ cups, divided

vanilla bean
1, split

yolks from large eggs
4

granulated sugar
¾ cup

1. Have ready an ice cream maker. Put 1½ cups of the half-and-half and the vanilla bean in a medium saucepan. Cook over medium heat until just boiling. Slide the pan from the heat, cover, and set aside for 15 minutes or up to 1 hour. Scoop out the bean and, using a small knife, scrape the seeds into the half-and-half.

2. Put the yolks and sugar in a medium bowl; whisk until well blended. Return the half-and-half to a simmer then slowly add to the yolk mixture, whisking constantly, until blended. Pour the yolk mixture back into the saucepan; cook over low heat, stirring constantly (including the sides and bottom), until the custard is thick enough to coat the back of a spoon and hold a line drawn through it or when it reaches 175° to 180°F on an instant-read thermometer, 4 to 6 minutes. Pour into a clean bowl and stir in the remaining 1¼ cups half-and-half. Let cool completely, then refrigerate until chilled, about 3 hours, or for up to 1 day. For faster cooling, set the bowl over a bowl filled with ice and stir occasionally until well chilled.

3. Arrange a 4½ x 8¼-inch loaf pan in the freezer, making sure it's level and secure. Pour the chilled mixture into the ice cream maker and process according to the manufacturer's instructions. Serve immediately (it will be soft) or scrape into the chilled dish, cover, and freeze until firm, about 1 hour, or for up to 2 days.

Switch-Ins

In place of the vanilla bean, switch in one of the following and strain before making the custard:
• fresh ginger, 2-inch piece, peeled and thinly sliced
• coffee beans, 1 cup

In place of the vanilla bean, switch in one of the following and add after making the custard:
• pure vanilla extract, 1½ teaspoons

Red Berry–Vanilla Ice Cream Bombe

SERVES 6 TO 8

raspberry sorbet
2 pints

**strawberry
ice cream**
1 pint

vanilla ice cream
1 pint

frozen strawberries
in syrup,
2 packages (10 ounces
each), thawed

1. Lightly grease a 2-quart round bowl with cooking spray. Line the bottom and sides with 2 long pieces of plastic wrap, letting the excess hang over the sides. Arrange the bowl in the freezer, making sure it's level and secure.

2. Remove the raspberry sorbet from the freezer and let soften at room temperature until just barely spreadable. Remove the bowl from the freezer. Using a rubber spatula, spread the sorbet in an even layer in the bottom of the bowl. Return the bowl to the freezer.

3. Remove the strawberry ice cream from the freezer and let soften at room temperature until just barely spreadable. Remove the bowl from the freezer. Using a rubber spatula, spread the ice cream in an even layer over the firm raspberry sorbet. Return the bowl to the freezer.

4. Remove the vanilla ice cream from the freezer and let soften at room temperature until just barely spreadable. Remove the bowl from the freezer. Using a rubber spatula, spread the vanilla ice cream over the strawberry ice cream. Cover with plastic wrap. Return the bowl to the freezer and freeze until hard before serving, about 6 hours, or for up to 3 days.

5. Pile the thawed strawberries and syrup into a food processor. Process until blended, about 20 seconds. Strain the sauce through a fine-mesh sieve into a small bowl, pressing firmly on the berries. Discard the pulp and seeds and use immediately or cover and refrigerate for up to 2 days.

6. To serve, unwrap the mold and invert onto a shallow serving plate. Gently pull on the plastic while lifting off the bowl. Cut into wedges and serve with a drizzle of sauce.

Switch-Ins
In place of the raspberry sorbet and strawberry and vanilla ice creams, switch in any flavors you like.

Basil Ice Cream

SERVES 4 TO 6

half-and-half
2½ cups, divided

fresh basil leaves
large, 8, torn into pieces

yolks from large eggs
4

granulated sugar
¾ cup

1. Have ready an ice cream maker. Put 1½ cups of the half-and-half and the basil in a medium saucepan. Cook over medium heat until just boiling. Slide the pan from the heat, cover, and set aside for 15 minutes or up to 1 hour. Pour into a blender and process until smooth, about 20 seconds.

2. Put the yolks and sugar in a medium bowl and whisk until well blended and pale in color. Return the half-and-half to the saucepan and bring to a simmer, then slowly add to the yolk mixture, whisking constantly, until blended. Pour the yolk mixture back into the saucepan and cook over low heat, stirring constantly (including the sides and bottom), until the custard is thick enough to coat the back of a spoon and hold a line drawn through it or when it reaches 175° to 180°F on an instant-read thermometer, 4 to 6 minutes. Pour into a clean bowl and stir in the remaining 1 cup half-and-half. Let cool completely, then refrigerate until chilled, about 3 hours, or for up to 1 day. For faster cooling, set the bowl over a bowl filled with ice and stir occasionally until well chilled.

3. Arrange a 4½ x 8¼-inch loaf pan in the freezer, making sure it's level and secure. Pour the chilled mixture into the ice cream maker and process according to the manufacturer's instructions. Serve immediately (it will be soft) or scrape into the chilled dish, cover, and freeze until firm, about 1 hour, or for up to 2 days.

Switch-Ins
In place of the basil, switch in one of the following:
• ground cinnamon, 1 teaspoon
• dried lavender, chopped, 1 tablespoon

Gussy It Up
Garnish with lemon basil leaves and lemon zest or chopped pistachios.

Toasted Coconut Ice Cream

SERVES 4 TO 6

coconut milk
1 can (14 ounces)

granulated sugar
1 cup

half-and-half
1 cup

sweetened shredded coconut
½ cup, toasted (see page 184 for more info)

1. Have ready an ice cream maker.

2. Put the coconut milk and sugar in a small saucepan. Cook, stirring, over medium heat until the sugar is dissolved. Slide the pan from the heat. Add the half-and-half and stir until well blended. Set aside to cool completely, then refrigerate until chilled, about 3 hours, or for up to 1 day. For faster cooling, set the bowl over a bowl filled with ice and stir occasionally until well chilled.

3. Arrange a 4½ x 8¼-inch loaf pan in the freezer, making sure it's level and secure. Pour the chilled mixture into the ice cream maker and process according to the manufacturer's instructions. Add the toasted coconut to the just-churned ice cream and mix until just blended. Serve immediately (it will be soft) or scrape into the chilled dish, cover, and freeze until firm, about 1 hour, or for up to 2 days.

Switch-Ins
In place of the toasted coconut, switch in one of the following and add just before the ice cream is finished:
• mini chocolate chips, ½ cup
• cookies (Oreo, gingersnap, coconut), crumbled, ½ cup

Gussy It Up
Serve with one of the caramel sauces (page 179), Killer Chocolate Sauce (page 179), Double Whole Berry Sauce (page 178), or Ruby Red Cranberry Sauce (page 179) and additional toasted coconut.

Apple Grape 'sicles

MAKES 4 ICE POPS

red grapes
seedless,
½ cup

green grapes
seedless,
½ cup

apple juice
⅓ cup

purple grape juice
⅓ cup

1. Have ready four 5- to 6-ounce ice pop molds and make room in the freezer, making sure the molds are level and secure.

2. Pile the red and green grapes into a food processor and pulse briefly until coarsely chopped. Spoon an equal amount of grapes into the molds.

3. Put the apple and grape juices in a small bowl or pitcher and mix until blended. Pour an equal amount of the juice mixture into the molds to cover the chopped grapes. Cover each mold with foil and push a wooden ice pop stick through the foil and into the middle of each pop. Freeze until firm, about 2 hours, or for up to 3 days.

4. To serve, remove the foil and slip the ice pops from the molds.

Switch-Ins
In place of the grapes, switch in the following:
• cherries, chopped, 1 cup (use half white and half red)

In place of the purple grape juice, switch in the following:
• white grape juice, ⅓ cup

Change It Up
In place of the ice pop molds, spoon the grapes and fruit juices into four 5-ounce paper cups. Cover each cup with foil and freeze until firm.

Icy Fruit Rockets

MAKES 4 ICE POPS

cran-raspberry juice cocktail
⅓ cup

fresh orange juice
½ cup

pineapple juice
½ cup

pomegranate juice
½ cup

1. Have ready four 5- or 6-ounce ice pop molds and make room in the freezer, making sure the molds are level and secure.

2. Pour an equal amount of the cran-raspberry juice into each mold. Cover each with foil and push a wooden ice pop stick through the foil and into the middle of the pops. Freeze until firm, 45 to 60 minutes.

3. Remove the molds from the freezer and carefully lift off the foil, leaving the sticks in the cups. Pour an equal amount of orange juice into each mold. Re-cover and freeze until firm, 45 to 60 minutes. Repeat layering and freezing with the pineapple juice and pomegranate juice. Freeze until firm, about 4 hours, or for up to 3 days.

4. To serve, remove the foil and slip the ice pops from molds.

Switch-Ins
In place of the fruit juices, switch in any flavored juice, fruit yogurt, or cider you like.

Change It Up
In place of the ice pop molds, pour the fruit juices into four 5-ounce paper cups, freezing each layer before adding another. Cover each cup with foil and freeze until firm.

Banana-Caramel Swirl Frozen Yogurt

SERVES 4

bananas
medium, very ripe,
2 (6 ounces each), peeled

plain yogurt
(preferably Greek style),
2 cups

brown sugar
1 cup, firmly packed

caramel topping
⅓ cup

1. Have ready an ice cream maker. Arrange a 4½ x 8¼-inch loaf pan in the freezer, making sure it's level and secure.

2. Pile the bananas, yogurt, and brown sugar into a food processor. Process until smooth, about 1 minute. Taste and add more brown sugar, if needed.

3. Pour the mixture into the ice cream maker and process according to the manufacturer's instructions. Swirl the caramel topping into the just-churned frozen yogurt. Serve immediately (it will be soft) or scrape into the chilled dish, cover, and freeze until firm, about 1 hour, or for up to 2 days.

Switch-Ins
In place of the brown sugar, switch in the following:
• granulated sugar, 1 cup

In place of the caramel topping, switch in one of the following:
• fudge topping, ⅓ cup
• cashews, chopped, ½ cup, toasted
• bittersweet chocolate, chopped, ½ cup

Gussy It Up
Serve with Chocolate Whipped Cream (page 180) or Killer Chocolate Sauce (page 179).

Triple Ginger Ice Cream Sandwiches

SERVES 4

vanilla ice cream
1 pint

crystallized ginger
chopped,
⅔ cup

ground ginger
1 teaspoon

ginger cookies
soft 3 inch,
8

1. Position a small cookie sheet in the freezer so that it lays flat.

2. Scoop the ice cream into a medium bowl. Add the crystallized ginger and ground ginger. Using a large spoon, mash the ingredients together until almost blended. If the ice cream is very soft, pop the bowl into the freezer for a few minutes to firm up.

3. Arrange 4 cookies, flat side up, on the counter. Using a ¼-cup ice cream scoop, divide the semi-firm ice cream mixture evenly onto the cookies. Top with the remaining cookies, flat side down. Press slightly to spread the ice cream to the edges. Arrange on the cookie sheet in the freezer and chill until firm. Serve immediately or wrap in plastic and store in the freezer until ready to serve, for up to 1 month.

Switch-Ins
In place of the vanilla ice cream, gingers, and cookies, switch in one of the following combinations:
• caramel ice cream, chopped peanut brittle, and oatmeal cookies
• vanilla ice cream, candied orange, finely grated orange zest, and chocolate wafer cookies
• chocolate ice cream, chopped fresh cherries, chopped pistachios, and chocolate wafer cookies

Gussy It Up
Roll the outside edge of the ice cream sandwiches in one of the following:
• shaved chocolate
• mini chocolate chips
• crushed peppermint hard candies
• chopped nuts, toasted
• colored sprinkles

Mulled Pear Cider Sorbet

SERVES 4 TO 6

pear cider
5 cups

mulling spices
2 teaspoons

granulated sugar
⅔ cup

pear liqueur
(Poire William),
2 tablespoons

1. Have ready an ice cream maker.

2. Put the cider and mulling spices in a large saucepan. Bring to a boil over high heat and boil until the liquid is reduced to $3\frac{1}{3}$ cups, about 10 minutes. Add the sugar and pear liqueur and stir until dissolved. Strain the liquid through a fine-mesh sieve into a clean bowl. Set aside to cool completely or refrigerate for up to 1 day. For faster cooling, set the bowl over a bowl filled with ice and stir occasionally until well chilled.

3. Arrange a $4\frac{1}{2}$ x $8\frac{1}{4}$-inch loaf pan in the freezer, making sure it's level and secure. Pour the chilled mixture into the ice cream maker and process according to the manufacturer's instructions. Serve immediately (it will be soft) or scrape into the chilled dish, cover, and freeze until firm, about 1 hour, or for up to 2 days.

Switch-Ins
In place of the pear liqueur, switch in the following:
• fresh lemon juice, 1 tablespoon

Change It Up
In place of the ice cream maker, arrange a 9 x 13-inch baking dish or $9\frac{1}{2}$-cup rectangular plastic container (Ziploc) in the freezer, making sure it's level and secure. Follow the directions for making the mixture. Pour the chilled mixture into the baking dish and freeze for about 2 hours. After that, every 30 minutes, stir, smash, and scrape the mixture with a table fork until the ice crystals are loose and frozen.

Ripe,
fresh fruit is nature's own
fast food. It's already sweetened, it's loaded
with flavor, it has interesting textures, and it's the perfect
building block for intriguing desserts. All that's needed are a few
flavor boosters and enhancers and dessert is ready. ※ Use the ripest, in-
season fruit available to you and buy local whenever possible. If the primary
fruit doesn't look so hot, check out the recommendations in "Switch-Ins" and sub
in the best fruit candidate. To expand a recipe's repertoire even further, keep in mind

fruit desserts

the type and texture of the original fruit called for in a recipe and swap in a similar one.
※ All fruit, even the ones you'll be peeling, should be rinsed and completely dried
before proceeding with a recipe. When handling berries, pick through them,
discarding any leaves and stems, as well as any bruised or moldy berries.
Put the berries in a colander and rinse with cold water. Line a baking
sheet with several layers of paper towels or a clean kitchen towel
and arrange the berries in an even layer. Cover with more
towels and pat dry.

Honey-Glazed Roasted Pears

SERVES 4

pears
(not Asian), ripe,
2

honey
⅓ cup

lemon zest
finely grated,
½ teaspoon

pure vanilla extract
½ teaspoon

1. Arrange an oven rack about 5 inches from the broiler and heat the broiler on high. Line a rimmed baking sheet with foil.

2. Cut the pears in half lengthwise and scoop out the core and seeds. Arrange the pear halves, cut side up, on the prepared baking sheet.

3. In a small ramekin, stir the honey, lemon zest, and vanilla. Spoon evenly into each pear half.

4. Broil the pears, rotating the pan once, until bubbling and caramelized, about 5 minutes. Serve warm.

Switch-Ins
In place of the lemon zest, switch in one of the following:
• ground cardamom, ¼ teaspoon
• ground cinnamon, ¼ teaspoon
• dark rum or brandy, 1 tablespoon

Gussy It Up
Serve the pear halves warm with vanilla ice cream or a dollop of Classic Sweetened Whipped Cream (page 180) or Ruby Red Cranberry Sauce (page 179) and sprinkle with toasted chopped pistachios.

Rum-Spiked Roasted Rhubarb–Strawberry Parfaits

SERVES 4

strawberries
1 quart (1 pound), rinsed, dried, and hulled

rhubarb
¾ pound, rinsed, dried, and trimmed

brown sugar
¾ cup, firmly packed

dark rum
1 tablespoon

1. Heat the oven to 425°F. Have ready an 8-inch-square baking dish. Cut the strawberries into quarters or, if large, into eighths. Cover and refrigerate until ready to serve.

2. Cut the rhubarb into 1½-inch pieces. Put in the baking dish and add the brown sugar. Toss until combined, then spread into a single layer. Bake, stirring twice, until the sauce is bubbling and the rhubarb is tender, about 15 minutes. Add the rum and stir gently until combined. Use immediately or cover and refrigerate until ready to serve.

3. To serve, reheat the rhubarb until warm, if necessary. Line up 4 parfait glasses or wineglasses. Beginning and ending with the prepared strawberries, evenly layer the strawberries and the rhubarb into the glasses. Serve immediately.

Switch-Ins
In place of the brown sugar, switch in the following:
• granulated sugar, ¾ cup

In place of the dark rum, switch in one or more of the following:
• ground cinnamon, ½ teaspoon
• orange zest, finely grated, 1 tablespoon

Gussy It Up
Serve topped with Vanilla Reduced Cream Sauce (page 179), vanilla ice cream, or a dollop of Classic Sweetened Whipped Cream (page 180) and a mint sprig.

Blueberry Orange Summer Pudding

SERVES 4 TO 6

blueberries
6 cups or 4 pints
(10 ounces each),
rinsed and dried

navel orange
medium, 1

granulated sugar
1⅓ cups

soft ladyfingers
2 packages (3 ounces
each), or 4 dozen

1. Set aside a few of the blueberries for garnish, if desired. Lightly grease a small (4-cup) bowl with cooking spray. Line with 2 long pieces of plastic wrap, letting the excess hang over the sides. Make room in the fridge.

2. Finely grate 2 teaspoons zest from the orange. Squeeze ⅔ cup juice from the orange. Put the juice and zest in a medium saucepan with about two-thirds of the blueberries and the sugar. Bring to a boil over medium heat, stirring. Reduce the heat to low and simmer, stirring, until the berries are soft and the liquid is syrupy, about 3 minutes. Slide the pan from the heat and add the remaining blueberries. With the back of a spoon, press on the fresh blueberries until lightly crushed. Set aside to cool slightly.

3. Arrange one row of ladyfingers top side down and slightly overlapping (keep attached, if possible) to cover the interior of the bowl completely. Fill gaps with smaller pieces. Spoon the berries (with as little liquid as possible) into the bowl. Cover with the remaining ladyfingers, then pour the juice on top. Wrap the excess plastic over the bowl. Put a flat plate large enough to cover the pudding on top and set a 2- or 3-pound weight (think large can of tomatoes) on it. Refrigerate for at least 8 hours or up to 2 days.

4. To serve, unwrap the mold and invert onto a shallow serving bowl or plate. Gently pull on the plastic while lifting off the bowl. Cut into wedges. Garnish with the reserved blueberries, if you like.

Switch-Ins
In place of the orange zest, switch in one of the following:
• ground cinnamon, ½ teaspoon
• lemon zest, finely grated, 2 teaspoons

In place of the ladyfingers, switch in the following:
• firm white bread, 24 crustless slices, about ¼ inch thick, halved

Strawberry Ginger Summer Pudding

SERVES 4 TO 6

strawberries
2 quarts (2 pounds),
rinsed, dried, and hulled

granulated sugar
1 cup

pound cake
1 (10¾-ounce) loaf,
thawed if frozen, brown
edges trimmed

crystallized ginger
finely chopped,
2 tablespoons

1. Lightly grease a small (4-cup) bowl with cooking spray. Line with 2 long pieces of plastic wrap; let the excess hang over the sides. Make room in the fridge.

2. Cut the berries into quarters or, if large, into eighths. Put the berries, sugar, and ²/₃ cup water in a medium saucepan. Bring to a boil over medium heat, stirring. Reduce the heat to low and simmer, stirring until the berries are tender and the liquid is syrupy, about 3 minutes. Set aside to cool slightly.

3. Cut the pound cake into thin (¼-inch) slices. Arrange slightly overlapping to cover the interior of the bowl. Fill any gaps with smaller pieces.

4. Stir the crystallized ginger into the berries. Spoon the berries (with as little juice as possible) into the lined bowl, cover with the remaining pound cake, then pour the juice on top. Wrap the excess plastic over the bowl. Put a flat plate large enough to cover the pudding on top and set a 2- or 3-pound weight (think large can of tomatoes) on it. Refrigerate for at least 8 hours or up to 2 days.

5. To serve, unwrap the mold and invert onto a shallow serving bowl or plate. Gently pull on the plastic while lifting off the bowl. Cut into wedges.

Switch-Ins
In place of the granulated sugar, switch in the following:
• brown sugar, 1⅓ cups, firmly packed

In place of the pound cake, switch in one of the following:
• firm white bread, 24 crustless slices, about ¼ inch thick, halved
• soft ladyfingers, 2 packages (3 ounces each), or 4 dozen

In place of the crystallized ginger, switch in one of the following:
• lemon zest, finely grated, 2 teaspoons
• orange zest, finely grated, 1 tablespoon

Grilled Pineapple Mint Julep Spears

SERVES 4

fresh mint leaves
¼ cup thinly sliced + 4
small sprigs for garnish

granulated sugar
2 tablespoons

bourbon
2 tablespoons

**fresh whole
pineapple**
1

1. Heat the grill to medium.

2. Put the ¼ cup sliced mint leaves, the sugar, and bourbon in a small bowl. Stir, pressing against the mint, until the sugar is dissolved. Set aside or cover and refrigerate for up to 1 day before continuing with the recipe. (If the syrup is refrigerated, warm it gently before serving.)

3. Using a serrated knife, remove the top and a thin slice of the base from the pineapple. Stand the pineapple on one end and cut away all the skin and brown spots, then cut the flesh into quarters lengthwise. Turn the pineapple quarters on a flat side and cut out most of the core. Cut each quarter in half lengthwise to make 8 long spears.

4. Put the pineapple spears on the hot grill. Cook, turning, until they're caramelized on each side, about 4 minutes. Arrange the pineapple spears on dessert plates and drizzle with the warm syrup. Garnish with the mint sprigs and serve immediately.

Switch-Ins
In place of the whole pineapple, switch in the following:
• fresh peeled, cored pineapple, store bought, 1

Change It Up
Instead of grilling, roast the pineapple. Arrange an oven rack about 3 inches from the broiler and heat the broiler on high. Line a rimmed baking sheet with foil. Broil the pineapple, turning the spears, until caramelized, about 5 minutes.

Sliced Pineapple with Reduced Ginger Drizzle and Toasted Coconut

SERVES 4

granulated sugar
¾ cup

fresh ginger
one 2-inch piece
(2 ounces), peeled and
very thinly sliced

fresh whole pineapple
1

sweetened shredded coconut
⅓ cup, toasted (see
page 184 for more info)

1. Put the sugar, 1 cup water, and the ginger slices in a small saucepan. Cook over medium heat until boiling. Reduce the heat to medium low and simmer, stirring occasionally, until syrupy and reduced to ¾ cup, about 10 to 12 minutes. Set aside to cool or cover and refrigerate for up to 3 days before continuing with the recipe.

2. Using a serrated knife, remove the top and a thin slice of the base from the pineapple. Stand the pineapple on one end and cut away all the skin and brown spots. Turn the pineapple on its side and cut into thin (¼-inch) slices. Use a small round cookie cutter to remove the core from each slice. Cover with plastic wrap and refrigerate until ready to serve, or arrange the pineapple slices, overlapping, on individual plates. Reheat the ginger syrup if necessary, and spoon 2 tablespoons over the slices, sprinkle with toasted coconut, and serve immediately.

Switch-Ins
In place of the fresh ginger, switch in one of the following:
- vanilla bean, 1, split in half lengthwise
- orange zest, finely chopped, 1 tablespoon
- lemon zest, finely chopped, 2 teaspoons

In place of the shredded coconut, switch in one the following:
- hazelnuts, chopped, ½ cup, toasted
- pistachios, chopped, ½ cup, toasted
- crystallized ginger, finely chopped, ¼ cup

Gussy It Up
Grill or broil the pineapple slices until warmed. Top with Whipped Mascarpone Cream (page 180) and drizzle with the ginger syrup.

Warm Apricot Halves
with Double Ginger Crumble

SERVES 4

gingersnap cookie crumbs
½ cup

unsalted butter
2 tablespoons, at room temperature

crystallized ginger
finely chopped,
1 tablespoon

apricots
ripe, 4, rinsed and dried

1. Heat the oven to 425°F. Have ready an 8-inch-square baking dish.

2. Put the cookie crumbs, butter, and crystallized ginger in a small bowl. Mix with a rubber spatula until well blended.

3. Cut the apricots in half, remove the pits, and arrange, cut side up, in the baking dish. Shape the crumb mixture into eight 1-tablespoon mounds and gently press into the center of each apricot. Bake until the apricots are just tender and hot, 8 to 10 minutes. Carefully transfer to 4 small serving plates and serve hot or warm.

Switch-Ins

In place of the gingersnap crumbs, switch in the following:
• chocolate cookie crumbs, ½ cup

In place of the apricots, switch in the following:
• medium, ripe peaches, 4

Gussy It Up
• Serve with vanilla ice cream or a dollop of Classic Sweetened Whipped Cream (page 180) or Whipped Mascarpone Cream (page 180) and a mint sprig.
• Drizzle with a little honey or spoon over one of the caramel sauces (page 179) or Easy Butterscotch Sauce (pages 178–179).

Classic Baked Apples

SERVES 4

brown sugar
¼ cup, firmly packed

unsalted butter
2 tablespoons, at room
temperature

ground cinnamon
½ teaspoon

apples
medium, 4, peeled

1. Heat the oven to 400°F. Have ready an 8-inch-square baking dish.

2. Put the brown sugar, butter, and cinnamon in a small bowl. Mix with a rubber spatula until well blended.

3. Cut off the top third of each apple and, using a small paring knife, cut out the core and seeds, leaving the bottom intact. Arrange the apples, top up, in the baking dish and add ⅓ cup water to the baking dish. Divide the brown sugar mixture into 4 equal piles and gently press into the center of each apple.

4. Bake until the apples are just tender, 30 to 45 minutes. Carefully transfer to small serving bowls, along with some of the liquid. Serve hot or warm.

Switch-Ins
In place of the cinnamon, switch in the following:
• ground ginger, ½ teaspoon

Gussy It Up
• Serve with a small scoop of vanilla ice cream or Vanilla Reduced Cream Sauce (page 179) or Boozy Hard Sauce (page 178).
• Bake the apples with pear or apple cider instead of the water.

Warm Maple Cranberry Pears

SERVES 4

whole cranberries
fresh or frozen,
1⅓ cups, rinsed and dried

pure maple syrup
(dark amber),
1 cup

dried cranberries
½ cup

ripe pears
(not Asian),
2

1. Put the fresh or frozen cranberries, maple syrup, and dried cranberries in a medium saucepan. Cook over medium heat until boiling. Reduce the heat to medium low and simmer, stirring occasionally, until the berries have popped, about 4 to 6 minutes. Set aside to cool slightly or transfer to a bowl, cover, and refrigerate for up to 3 days before reheating and serving.

2. Peel the pears and cut in half lengthwise. Scoop out the core and seeds.

3. Arrange 1 pear half on each serving plate. Spoon the warm cranberries over the pear. Repeat with the remaining ingredients and serve immediately.

Switch-Ins
In place of the dried cranberries, switch in one or more of the following:
• dried apricots, chopped, ½ cup
• crystallized ginger, chopped, ¼ cup
• pecans, chopped, ½ cup, toasted (add just before serving)

In place of the ripe pears, switch in the following:
• canned pear halves, 4, drained

Gussy It Up
• Put the pear halves on a cutting board, cut side down. Cut into ¼-inch-thick lengthwise slices, keeping the slices lined up together. Arrange 1 pear half on each serving plate and carefully fan the slices and top with warm compote.
• Serve with a scoop of vanilla ice cream or a drizzle of one of the caramel sauces (page 179).

Citrus Pomegranate Terrine

SERVES 6 TO 8

grapefruits
4

navel oranges
large, 4

gelatin
unflavored powder,
2 envelopes

pomegranate seeds
¼ cup

1. Have ready a 4½ x 8¼-inch loaf pan. Make room in the fridge. Cut off the ends of the grapefruits and oranges. Position the fruit on one end and cut away all the zest and pith, following the fruits' contours. Holding the fruit in one hand over a large bowl, cut along the membranes to release the sections into the bowl. Squeeze the juice from the membranes into a 2-cup measure. Pour off enough of the juice to measure 1¾ cups; discard (or drink) the remainder.

2. Pour ¾ cup of the juice into a small, heatproof bowl and sprinkle the gelatin on top. Let sit until the gelatin is moist, about 3 minutes. Microwave until the gelatin is dissolved and the liquid is clear, 30 to 90 seconds. Add to the remaining 1 cup juice and set aside to cool slightly.

3. Add the pomegranate seeds to the citrus sections and gently toss to combine. Pile the mixture evenly into the loaf pan, leaving behind any extra juices. Slowly pour the warm (not hot) gelatin liquid over the sections. Tap the loaf pan gently on the counter to release any air bubbles. Refrigerate until the top is set and then cover with plastic. Refrigerate until firm, about 6 hours, or for up to 2 days.

4. To serve, run a small knife between the gelatin and the pan and dip the bottom of the pan into warm water for about 1 minute. Invert onto a flat plate and shake gently to loosen the terrine. Cut into 1-inch slices.

Switch-Ins
In place of the pomegranate seeds, switch in the following:
• fresh mint leaves, thinly sliced, 2 tablespoons

Gussy It Up
• Serve with Double Whole Berry Sauce (page 178).
• Garnish with fresh mint sprigs.
• Use a combination of white and ruby red grapefruit.

Rum-Raisin Bananas Foster

SERVES 4 TO 6

bananas
ripe, 4, peeled

unsalted butter
4 tablespoons, divided

brown sugar
½ cup, firmly packed

**rum-raisin
ice cream**
1 pint

1. Cut the bananas on a sharp diagonal into ³/₄-inch slices.

2. Put 2 tablespoons of the butter in a large skillet. Melt over medium-high heat, stirring frequently, until bubbling. Add the banana slices, cut side down, and cook, turning to brown both sides, about 1 minute per side. Slide the skillet from the heat and, leaving the butter in the skillet, transfer the bananas to a medium bowl. Cover loosely with foil.

3. Add the remaining 2 tablespoons butter, the brown sugar, and ½ cup water to the skillet. Bring to a boil, scraping up the nubbins on the skillet, over medium-high heat and cook until the sauce is brown and bubbling slowly, about 2 to 2½ minutes. Slide the skillet from the heat. Put the bananas back into the skillet to reheat and toss gently in the sauce. Serve immediately with rum-raisin ice cream.

Switch-Ins
In place of the rum-raisin ice cream, switch in one or both of the following:
• French vanilla ice cream, 1 pint
• pound cake, 4 to 6 slices, lightly toasted

Gussy It Up
• Stir ¼ teaspoon ground cinnamon into the sauce along with the water.
• Serve with sliced pound cake, angel food cake, or soft ladyfingers.
• Substitute 2 tablespoons dark rum for 2 tablespoons of the water and proceed as directed.

Flash-Roasted Fruit Compote

SERVES 4

fresh fruit
(assorted),
6 cups, cut up in
similar sizes

brown sugar
½ cup, firmly packed

fresh lemon juice
2 tablespoons

pistachios
chopped,
½ cup

1. Heat the oven to 425°F. Have ready a 9 x 13-inch baking dish.

2. Put the fruit, sugar, and lemon juice in the baking dish and toss gently until combined. Spread in a single layer. Roast, stirring twice, until the sauce is bubbling and the fruit is just tender and beginning to release its juices, about 12 minutes. Stir gently until combined.

3. To serve, spoon the warm compote into four parfait glasses or wineglasses and sprinkle with the chopped pistachios. Serve immediately.

Switch-Ins
In place of the brown sugar, switch in the following:
• granulated sugar, ½ cup

In place of the pistachios, switch in one of the following:
• Hazelnuts, pecans or macadamia nuts, chopped, ½ cup, toasted

Gussy It Up
• Serve with vanilla ice cream or a dollop of Classic Sweetened Whipped Cream (page 180) or Whipped Mascarpone Cream (page 180) and a mint sprig.
• Serve with one of the caramel sauces (page 179) or Easy Butterscotch Sauce (pages 178–179).
• Serve with crisp ginger cookies or pound cake slices, lightly toasted.

Maple-Glazed Figs
with Hazelnut Mascarpone

SERVES 4

mascarpone
⅔ cup

pure maple syrup
(grade A dark amber),
5 tablespoons, divided

figs
large, ripe, 6, rinsed
and dried

hazelnuts
chopped,
¼ cup, toasted

1. Put the mascarpone and 4 tablespoons of the maple syrup in a small bowl and stir until blended. Cover and refrigerate until ready to serve or for up to 4 days.

2. Arrange an oven rack about 5 inches from the broiler and heat the broiler on high. Line a rimmed baking sheet with foil.

3. Cut the figs in half lengthwise. Arrange, cut side up, on the prepared baking sheet and drizzle with the remaining 1 tablespoon maple syrup. Broil the figs, rotating the pan once, until bubbling and caramelized, about 3 minutes.

4. To serve, arrange the warm figs (3 per person) on small plates. Drizzle with any accumulated juices in the baking sheet. Serve the warm figs with the maple mascarpone and sprinkle with the hazelnuts.

Switch-Ins
In place of the maple syrup, switch in the following:
• brown sugar, 6 tablespoons, firmly packed (4 tablespoons for the mascarpone + 2 tablespoons for the figs)

In place of the hazelnuts, switch in one of the following:
• pistachios, chopped, ¼ cup, toasted
• walnuts, chopped, ¼ cup, toasted

Vanilla Orange Compote

SERVES 4

navel oranges
large, 6, divided

lemon
1

vanilla bean
½

granulated sugar
⅔ cup

1. Have ready a shallow bowl or plate and make room in the fridge.

2. Cut 2 oranges in half and squeeze enough juice to measure 1 cup. Peel away one long piece of lemon zest and remove any white pith with a paring knife. Cut the lemon in half and squeeze out 3 tablespoons juice.

3. Pour both juices into a small saucepan. Using the tip of a knife, split the half vanilla bean down the length of the pod. Add the split bean, sugar, and lemon peel to the saucepan. Bring to a boil, reduce the heat to medium low, and simmer until reduced to ½ cup, about 8 minutes. Slide the pan from the heat, cover, and set aside for 10 minutes.

4. Cut off the ends of the remaining 4 oranges. Position each orange on one end and cut away all the zest and pith following the fruit's contours. Turn the orange on its side and cut into ¼-inch-thick slices. Arrange the slices in layers in the bowl or on the plate.

5. Fish out the lemon peel and vanilla bean from the syrup; discard the peel. Scrape the seeds from the bean and add to the syrup. Carefully pour the syrup over the orange slices, garnish with the vanilla bean on top, and serve immediately or cover and refrigerate for up to 4 hours.

Switch-Ins
In place of the navel oranges, switch in the following:
• blood oranges, 7 (2 for juice; 5 for slicing)

In place of the vanilla bean, switch in one of the following:
• fresh ginger, thinly sliced, ⅓ cup
• cinnamon stick, 1
• star anise pods, 3
• pure vanilla extract, ¾ teaspoon (add after cooking)

Sliced Mango with Crispy Ginger Sabayon

SERVES 6

mangos
medium, ripe,
3 (14 ounces each)

large eggs
2

brown sugar
¼ cup, firmly packed

gingersnap cookies
crushed,
¼ cup

1. Have ready 6 small dessert plates and make room in the fridge.

2. Using a peeler or small paring knife, peel the mangos. Turn each mango on its side and cut the halves away from the pit. If the mango is too slippery to hold, use a paper towel to steady it on the cutting board. Cut each half into thin slices and fan them out on the dessert plates. Set aside or cover and refrigerate for up to 6 hours before serving.

3. Put the eggs and brown sugar in a medium heatproof bowl. Whisk until blended. Set the bowl over simmering water. Using an electric hand-held mixer, beat the mixture on medium speed until very thick and glossy, about 5 minutes.

4. Spoon the sabayon evenly over one side of the mango fans and sprinkle the gingersnap cookie crumbs on top. Serve immediately.

Switch-Ins
In place of the mangos, switch in one of the following:
• very ripe bananas, 6 small, thinly sliced
• ripe peaches or nectarines, 4, pitted and sliced

In place of the brown sugar, switch in the following:
• granulated sugar, ¼ cup

In place of the crushed gingersnap cookies, switch in one of the following:
• crushed amaretti cookies, ¼ cup
• chopped pecans, ¼ cup, toasted
• macadamia nuts, chopped, ¼ cup, toasted
• sweetened shredded coconut, ⅓ cup, toasted

Gussy It Up
Add ¾ teaspoon pure vanilla extract or 2 teaspoons of dark rum, brandy, or orange-flavored liqueur to the cooked sabayon.

Orange-Glazed Grilled Peach Melba

SERVES 4

peaches
firm-ripe, 4, rinsed and
dried

fresh orange juice
1 cup

brown sugar
½ cup, firmly packed

raspberry sorbet
1 pint

1. Heat the grill to medium. Cut the peaches in half lengthwise and scoop out the pit. Put the orange juice in a small bowl or ramekin and the brown sugar on a small rimmed plate. Dip the cut side of the peach halves in orange juice and then in the brown sugar to make a thin coating. Arrange, cut side up, on a plate. Reserve the remaining orange juice and brown sugar.

2. Put the peaches, cut side down, on the hot grill. Cook until caramelized, about 3 minutes. Carefully turn over the peaches and continue grilling until tender, about 2 minutes.

3. Meanwhile, make the sauce. Put the remaining juice and brown sugar in a small saucepan. Bring to a boil over medium-high heat and boil, stirring occasionally, until reduced to about ⅓ cup, about 4 minutes.

4. Arrange the peach halves, cut side up, in shallow bowls (2 per bowl). Top the peaches with the raspberry sorbet and drizzle with the warm syrup. Serve immediately.

Switch-Ins
In place of the raspberry sorbet, switch in one of the following:
• vanilla ice cream, 1 pint
• pistachios, coarsely chopped, ¼ cup, toasted
• shaved chocolate, ½ cup

Gussy It Up
Add 1 tablespoon dark rum or orange-flavored liqueur to the warm sauce.

Change It Up
Instead of grilling the peaches, broil them in the oven. Arrange an oven rack about 5 inches from the broiler and heat the broiler on high. Line a rimmed baking sheet with foil. Broil the peaches, cut side up, rotating the pan once, until bubbling and caramelized, about 5 minutes.

Gingered Blackberry–Limoncello Sundaes

SERVES 4

blackberries
1½ pints (18 ounces),
rinsed and dried

crystallized ginger
finely chopped,
1 tablespoon

coconut sorbet
1 pint

limoncello
chilled,
½ cup

1. Have ready 4 large parfait glasses or wineglasses and make room in the fridge.

2. Put the blackberries and chopped ginger in a medium bowl and toss, crushing the berries slightly, until combined. Continue with the recipe or cover and refrigerate for up to 6 hours.

3. Just before serving, set the sorbet on the counter to soften slightly. Spoon about half of the berry mixture evenly into the glasses, add a scoop of the coconut sorbet, and top with the remaining berries and any remaining juices. Drizzle with the limoncello and serve immediately.

Switch-Ins

In place of the blackberries, switch in one the following:
• blueberries, 1 pint
• raspberries, 1 pint

In place of the coconut sorbet, switch in one of the following:
• mango sorbet, 1 pint
• lemon sorbet, 1 pint
• orange sorbet, 1 pint

In place of the limoncello, switch in one of the following:
• orange-flavored liqueur, ½ cup
• fresh orange juice, ½ cup

Melon Compote with
Honey Lavender Syrup

SERVES 6

cantaloupe
small, ripe,
1

honey
½ cup

fresh orange juice
3 tablespoons

dried lavender
1½ teaspoons

1. Have ready a shallow bowl or large plate and make room in the fridge.

2. Using a serrated knife, cut the cantaloupe in half lengthwise and scoop out the seeds. Cut each half into 4 or 6 wedges. Cut between the rind and the flesh of each slice and cut each wedge into ½-inch-thick slices. Casually arrange the slices in the bowl or on the plate. Cover with plastic wrap and refrigerate until ready to serve.

3. Put the honey, 1 cup water, the orange juice, and the lavender in a small saucepan. Bring to a boil, reduce the heat to medium, and cook until reduced to ⅔ cup, 8 to 10 minutes. Slide the pan from the heat, cover, and set aside for 10 to 15 minutes. Carefully pour the warm syrup over the cantaloupe slices and serve immediately, or cover and refrigerate for up to 6 hours. Warm the syrup before serving if needed.

Switch-Ins

In place of the cantaloupe, switch in one the following:
• firm-ripe peaches, 6, halved and pitted, each half cut into 3 wedges
• apricots, 6, halved and pitted, each half cut into 3 or 4 wedges

In place of the orange juice, switch in one of the following:
• fresh lemon juice, 1 tablespoon
• fresh lime juice, 1 tablespoon

In place of the dried lavender, switch in one of the following:
• lemon thyme sprigs, 2 small
• orange zest, finely grated, 1 tablespoon

Balsamic Strawberries and Melon

SERVES 4 TO 6

strawberries
1 quart (1 pound), rinsed, dried, and hulled

confectioners' sugar
¼ cup

balsamic vinegar
1 tablespoon

cantaloupe
small, ripe, 1

1. Cut the strawberries into halves or quarters, depending on their size. Put the berries, sugar, and vinegar in a medium bowl and toss gently to combine. Refrigerate, tossing occasionally, until just softened and juicy, 15 to 45 minutes (but no longer or the berries will be mushy).

2. Using a serrated knife, cut the cantaloupe in half lengthwise and scoop out the seeds. Cut each half into 4 or 6 wedges. Cut between the rind and the flesh of each slice but keep the rind and flesh together (this makes for easier eating). Cover with plastic wrap and refrigerate until ready to serve.

3. To serve, arrange the melon wedges upright on individual plates and sprinkle with a pinch of salt. Spoon the strawberries and some juice over the wedges and serve immediately.

Switch-Ins
In place of the strawberries, switch in one of the following:
• raspberries, 2 pints
• blackberries, 2 pints

In place of the balsamic vinegar, switch in one of the following:
• fresh lime juice, 1 tablespoon
• fresh orange juice, 2 tablespoons

Gussy It Up
• Serve with a sprinkle of finely chopped fresh mint or lemon basil.
• Serve the balsamic strawberries over lightly toasted pound cake with Classic Sweetened Whipped Cream (page 180) instead of the melon.

Sparkling Minty Grilled Watermelon

SERVES 6

fresh mint
chopped,
3 tablespoons

granulated sugar
3 tablespoons

**small seedless
watermelon**
(red or yellow),
1 (about 3 pounds)

Moscato d'Asti®
1 cup

1. Heat a very clean grill to medium high. Have ready a large plate or 6 individual dessert bowls.

2. Put the mint and sugar in a small bowl or mortar. Using the back of a spoon or a pestle, mash and smear the mint and sugar until well blended and the sugar is vibrant green. Set aside or cover and refrigerate for up to 1 day before serving.

3. Cut the watermelon into $1\frac{1}{2}$-inch chunks and discard the rind. Coat the pieces very lightly with cooking spray. Put the watermelon on the hot grill and cook until grill marks appear, about 2 minutes. Carefully turn the chunks and continue grilling until two sides are marked and the watermelon is warm. Arrange on the plate or in the bowls and sprinkle evenly with the mint-sugar mixture; gently toss until combined. The grilled watermelon can be served immediately or covered and refrigerated for up to 4 hours before serving.

4. Just before serving, pour the Moscato d'Asti evenly over the watermelon.

Switch-Ins
In place of the mint, switch in one of the following:
• crystallized ginger, finely chopped, 2 tablespoons
• orange zest, finely grated, 2 tablespoons

In place of the watermelon, switch in the following:
• firm-ripe peaches, 6, pitted and halved

In place of the Moscato d'Asti, switch in one of the following:
• muscat wine, 1 cup
• sparkling wine, 1 cup
• Prosecco, 1 cup

Lime-Scented Cherries and Apricot Halves

SERVES 4 TO 6

lime
1

cherries
¾ pound, rinsed and pitted

granulated sugar
½ cup

apricots
ripe, 4, rinsed and dried

1. Finely grate 1 teaspoon zest from the lime and set aside. Squeeze the juice from the lime and measure out 2 teaspoons. Put the juice and zest in a medium saucepan with about half of the cherries and the sugar.

2. Bring to a boil over medium heat, stirring frequently. Reduce the heat to low and simmer, stirring constantly, until the cherries are soft and the liquid is syrupy, about 3 minutes. Slide the pan from the heat and add the remaining cherries. Set aside to cool or transfer to a bowl, cover, and refrigerate for up to 4 hours before serving.

3. Cut the apricots in half and remove and discard the pit. If the apricots are large, cut each half into 2 wedges. Put the apricots in a large bowl and add the cooled cherry mixture. Toss until blended. Serve immediately in 4 small dessert bowls or cover and refrigerate for up to 1 day before serving chilled.

Switch-Ins
In place of the cherries, switch in the following:
• blueberries, 3 pints (12 ounces)

In place of the apricots, switch in the following:
• ripe peaches, 2, pitted and quartered

Gussy It Up
Serve with crisp cookies and one of the whipped creams (page 180).

Raspberry Nectarine Fruit-Tinis

SERVES 4

nectarines
ripe, 2 (10 ounces),
rinsed and dried

raspberries
1 pint (12 ounces), rinsed
and dried

orange zest
finely grated,
1 ½ teaspoons

Prosecco
chilled,
½ bottle

1. Have ready 4 large martini glasses or wineglasses and make room in the fridge.

2. Coarsely chop the nectarines. Put the nectarines, raspberries, and orange zest in a medium bowl and toss gently to combine. Spoon into the glasses, cover, and refrigerate until ready to serve or for up to 4 hours.

3. To serve, pour $^1/_4$ to $^1/_3$ cup chilled Prosecco over the fruit and serve immediately.

Switch-Ins

In place of the nectarines, switch in one of the following:
- peaches, 2
- kiwis, 2, peeled

In place of the raspberries, switch in one of the following:
- blueberries, 1 pint
- blackberries, 1 pint

In place of the orange zest, switch in one of the following:
- lemon zest, finely grated, ½ teaspoon
- fresh mint leaves, thinly sliced, 1 tablespoon
- fresh lemon basil, thinly sliced, 1 tablespoon

In place of the Prosecco, switch in one of the following:
- sparkling wine, ½ bottle
- champagne, ½ bottle

Home-baked
pies, cobblers, tarts, and
galettes are the pinnacle of baking, but
because most folks are too time-pressed or intimidated
to make pastry dough, these treasures are relegating to the
"read, drool, turn the page" category. This section will relieve any pie
anxiety you suffer from and have your home smelling of fresh baked pastry
and fruit in record time without sacrificing flavor and quality. ❋ When working with
pastry dough, shape it without pulling and stretching and work with it cold but pliable

pastry desserts

to avoid cracking. If the dough starts to get too warm, you risk losing flakiness and
layers, so slide it onto a cookie sheet and refrigerate for a few minutes until it chills out.
❋ Once you have made a recipe a few times with one dough, feel free to experiment with different types or brands of dough in place of the suggested
one. First check out the recipes that call for the new dough and see if it
requires special handling and then follow the directions, making any
changes as you go.

Banana–Brown Sugar Pie Pockets

SERVES 8

banana
medium, very ripe,
1, peeled

brown sugar
2 tablespoons, firmly
packed, divided

pure vanilla extract
½ teaspoon

premade pie dough
1 sheet, thawed

1. Heat the oven to 400°F. Line 1 large cookie sheet with a nonstick liner.

2. In a small bowl, mash the banana, 1 tablespoon of the brown sugar, and the vanilla with a fork until blended.

3. Carefully unfold or unroll the pie dough. Using a 4-inch round cookie cutter (or the bottom of a 29-ounce can of tomatoes as a guide) cut out 5 rounds. Peel away the scraps and pile them together. Using a rolling pin, roll the dough to a ¼-inch thickness. Cut out 3 more rounds.

4. Place about a tablespoon of the banana filling on the center of each round. Using your finger, brush the edge of the dough with water. Fold half of the dough over the filling to form a half-moon–shaped turnover. Using the tines of a fork, press the curved edge to seal tightly.

5. Arrange the pie pockets on the prepared cookie sheet, about 2 inches apart. Brush the tops with some water or spritz with cooking spray and sprinkle evenly with the remaining 1 tablespoon brown sugar. Bake until the pastry is puffed and browned, about 20 minutes. Serve warm.

Switch-Ins
In place of the vanilla, switch in one of the following:
• crystallized ginger, chopped, 2 tablespoons
• ground cinnamon, ½ teaspoon
• dark rum or brandy, 1 tablespoon
• chopped nuts, 2 tablespoons, toasted

Gussy It Up
Drizzle the pie pockets with Vanilla or Citrus Glaze (page 180) or pair with one or more of the following: a scoop or two of caramel swirl ice cream, Classic Sweetened Whipped Cream (page 180), a drizzle of one of the caramel sauces (page 179), or toasted nuts.

Maple Blueberry Pandowdy

SERVES 4 TO 6

blueberries
1½ pints (18 ounces),
rinsed and dried

all-purpose flour
1 tablespoon

**granulated maple
sugar**
⅔ cup, divided

premade pie dough
1 sheet, thawed

1. Put a small foil-lined baking sheet on the oven rack and heat the oven to 400°F. Have ready a 9-inch glass pie plate.

2. Put the blueberries, flour, and ½ cup of the maple sugar in a medium bowl. Toss gently until blended. Pile the mixture into the pie plate and spread evenly.

3. Carefully unfold or unroll the pie dough and lay it on top of the filling, letting the excess hang over the edges of the dish. Using your fingers, roll the excess dough under itself until the rolled dough sits on the edge of the dish. Using your index finger and thumb from one hand and the index finger of the opposite, crimp to make a scalloped edge that sits on top of the edge of the dish. Using a small, sharp knife, cut three 2-inch-long vents in the pie dough. Brush the dough with water and sprinkle evenly with the remaining maple sugar.

4. Carefully place the pandowdy on the hot baking sheet. Bake until the pastry is browned and the filling is bubbling, about 35 minutes. Serve warm.

Switch-Ins
In place of the blueberries, switch in one of the following:
• ripe apricots, 1¼ pounds, quartered and pitted
• ripe plums, 1¼ pounds, quartered and pitted

In place of the granulated maple sugar, switch in one of the following:
• granulated sugar, ⅔ cup
• brown sugar, ⅔ cup, firmly packed

Gussy It Up
Add one or more of the following to the filling before topping and baking:
• ground cinnamon, ½ teaspoon
• fresh lemon juice, 2 teaspoons
• orange zest, finely grated, 2 teaspoons

Serve with Boozy Hard Sauce (page 178) or Vanilla Reduced Cream Sauce (page 179).

Fruit-Filled Cocoa Meringue Shells

SERVES 4

confectioners' sugar
1½ cups

whites from large eggs
3

cocoa powder
3 tablespoons, sifted

assorted fresh fruit
diced,
2½ cups

1. Heat the oven to 350°F. Line 1 large cookie sheet with parchment.

2. Sift the confectioners' sugar twice to remove the lumps, divide into 2 equal portions, and set aside.

3. Put the egg whites and a pinch of salt in a medium bowl. Beat with an electric mixer on medium speed until foamy. Increase the speed to medium high and beat until the whites hold soft peaks. Continue beating and gradually add 1 portion of the sifted confectioners' sugar. Beat until firm and glossy peaks form. Add the sifted cocoa powder and beat briefly to combine. Using a large rubber spatula, fold in the remaining sugar.

4. Drop large scoopfuls of the meringue to form 4 equal mounds about 3 inches apart on the prepared cookie sheet. Using the back of a large spoon, hollow out the center of each mound to form 4-inch round meringue nests.

5. Reduce the oven temperature to 200°F. Bake until the meringues are only slightly sticky when pressed with a fingertip, about 1½ hours. Turn off the oven and let the meringues cool in the oven for 1 hour. Serve immediately, filled with the assorted fruit, or cover and store at room temperature for up to 2 days.

Switch-Ins
In place of the cocoa, switch in one of the following:
• lemon zest, finely grated, 1 teaspoon
• orange zest, finely grated, 2 teaspoons
• pure vanilla extract, ½ teaspoon

Gussy It Up
• Fill the nests with one or more of the following: a small scoop of vanilla ice cream, Classic Sweetened Whipped Cream (page 180), or toasted, chopped nuts.
• Drizzle with Killer Chocolate Sauce (page 179) or one of the caramel sauces (page 179).

Rustic Dried Fruit Tart

MAKES 1 TART; SERVES 4 TO 6

confectioners' sugar
½ cup, divided

mixed dried fruit
coarsely chopped,
2¼ cups (10½ ounces),
lightly packed

orange marmalade
½ cup

frozen puff pastry sheet
1 (about 9 ounces),
thawed

1. Heat the oven to 400°F. Line 1 rimmed baking sheet with a nonstick liner. Set aside 2 tablespoons of the confectioners' sugar.

2. Put the dried fruit, $^2/_3$ cup water, and the marmalade in a medium saucepan and cook over medium heat until boiling. Reduce the heat to low, cover, and simmer, stirring occasionally, until the fruit is tender and the liquid is reduced and thickened, about 10 minutes. Set aside to cool completely or transfer to a bowl, cover, and refrigerate for up to 3 days.

3. Arrange a large piece of plastic wrap on the counter. Sprinkle generously with some of the remaining confectioners' sugar. Using a rolling pin, roll out the puff pastry sheet, sprinkling the top and bottom often and generously with the sugar to prevent sticking, into a 10-inch square, then trim into a 10-inch round. Move to the prepared baking sheet.

4. Spoon the cooled dried fruit into the center of the pastry, mounding it slightly and leaving about a 2-inch border. Fold the edges over the filling, pleating the pastry as you go around the filling and leaving the center of the fruit uncovered. Sprinkle the remaining sugar over the pastry.

5. Bake until the pastry is golden brown, about 35 minutes. If the pastry puffs up, prick with a fork or knife tip. Set on a rack to cool slightly before serving.

Switch-Ins
In place of the mixed dried fruit, switch in the following:
• dried apricots, coarsely chopped, 1½ cups, lightly packed

In place of the orange marmalade, switch in the following:
• seedless raspberry jam, ½ cup

Gussy It Up
Serve with Boozy Hard Sauce (page 178) or vanilla ice cream.

Individual Peach Tarte Tatins

SERVES 4

peaches
medium, ripe,
2 (5 ounces each), rinsed
and dried

frozen puff pastry
sheet
1 (about 9 ounces),
thawed

brown sugar
¾ cup, firmly packed

ground cinnamon
1¼ teaspoons

1. Put a small, foil-lined baking sheet on the oven rack and heat the oven to 400°F. Lightly grease four 8-ounce ramekins. Cut the peaches in half lengthwise and remove the pit.

2. Unfold the puff pastry sheet on a work surface. Using a sharp knife and a ramekin as a guide, cut into 4 rounds slightly larger than the ramekin. Cover with plastic.

3. Blend the brown sugar and cinnamon in a small bowl. Portion the sugar mixture evenly into the ramekins. Put one peach half, skin side down, in each ramekin. Arrange a puff pastry round over each ramekin and press gently against the peach, leaving the edge of the pastry tucked against the inside edge of the ramekin.

4. Carefully arrange the ramekins on the hot baking sheet in the oven. Bake until the pastry is well browned, about 45 minutes. Set the baking sheet on a rack. Using a pot holder, invert each ramekin onto a small plate, keeping the ramekin in place for about 3 minutes to allow the sugar syrup to release from the ramekin. Lift off the ramekins and serve.

Switch-Ins
In place of the peaches, switch in one of the following:
• small apples or small, ripe pears, 2 (7 ounces each), peeled and cored
  (add 1 tablespoon water to each ramekin before adding fruit)
• medium, ripe nectarines, 2 (5 ounces each)

In place of the cinnamon, switch in one of the following:
• ground ginger, 1¾ teaspoons
• ground cardamom, ¾ teaspoon

Gussy It Up
Serve with one or more of the following: a scoop or two of maple or vanilla ice cream, Boozy Hard Sauce (page 178), Vanilla Reduced Cream Sauce (page 179), Classic Sweetened Whipped Cream (page 180), or toasted, chopped nuts.

Chocolate Hazelnut Pear Dumplings

SERVES 4

pears
medium, ripe, 2, rinsed
and dried

Nutella
⅓ cup

premade pie dough
2 sheets, thawed

hazelnuts
chopped,
⅓ cup

1. Heat the oven to 375°F. Line 1 large cookie sheet with a nonstick liner. Peel the pears and cut in half lengthwise. Using a small spoon or a melon baller, scoop out the core and enough flesh to make a well about 1 tablespoon in size. Portion the Nutella evenly into each well.

2. Carefully unfold or unroll both sheets of pie dough. Cut each round in half. Place a pear half, filling side down, on one half of each piece of dough. Brush the dough edge around the pear with water. Fold the other half of the dough over the pear to form a triangle-shaped dumpling, pressing the dough layers together. Cut away all but ¾ inch of the dough and, using the tines of a fork, press the edge to seal tightly.

3. Arrange the dumplings on the prepared cookie sheet about 2 inches apart. Using a small, sharp knife, cut 3 small vents in each dumpling. Brush the tops with some water or spritz with cooking spray and sprinkle evenly with the chopped hazelnuts, pressing lightly into the dough. Bake until the pastry is browned, 42 to 45 minutes. If the nuts begin to burn, cover loosely with foil. Serve warm.

Switch-Ins
In place of the pears, switch in the following:
• medium apples, 2, peeled, cut in half, and core removed

In place of the Nutella, switch in the following:
• caramels, 8 small squares, unwrapped (2 per fruit half)

In place of the hazelnuts, switch in the following:
• pecans or walnuts, chopped, ⅓ cup

Gussy It Up
Instead of brushing the dough with water before sprinkling with the nuts, use an egg wash (see page 182) for a glossy finish. Drizzle Vanilla or Citrus Glaze (page 180) over the baked and cooled tops.

Raspberry Peach Sugar Puffs

SERVES 4

granulated sugar
3 tablespoons, divided

frozen puff pastry sheet
1 (about 9 ounces), thawed

peach
medium, ripe,
1 (5 ounces), coarsely chopped,

raspberries
3 ounces, rinsed and dried

1. Heat the oven to 400°F. Lightly grease 4 muffin cups, leaving an empty cup in between. Set aside 1½ tablespoons of the sugar for garnish.

2. Using a sharp knife, cut the puff pastry sheet into 4 equal squares. Line the prepared muffin cups with the puff pastry squares, pressing them into the bottoms and up the sides, allowing the excess to hang over the edges.

3. Put the chopped peaches, raspberries, and remaining sugar in a small bowl. Toss gently to combine. Spoon the fruit evenly into the pastry cups. Fold the excess pastry over the tops or leave open-faced. Sprinkle the reserved sugar over the pastry.

4. Bake until the pastry is golden brown, about 25 minutes. Set on a rack to cool slightly, about 10 minutes, before serving.

Switch-Ins
In place of the granulated sugar, switch in the following:
• brown sugar, 3 tablespoons, firmly packed

In place of the peach, switch in one of the following:
• medium, ripe apricot, 1 (5 ounces), coarsely chopped
• medium, ripe nectarine, 1 (5 ounces), coarsely chopped

In place of the raspberries, switch in the following:
• blueberries, 3 ounces

Gussy It Up
• Add ½ teaspoon finely grated ginger to the fruit mixture.
• Serve with vanilla ice cream.

Raspberry Peach Galette

MAKES 1 GALETTE; SERVES 4 TO 6

seedless raspberry jam
½ cup, divided

peaches
ripe, 3 (1 pound total), rinsed, dried, and cut into 1-inch pieces

premade pie dough
1 sheet, thawed

turbinado sugar
2 tablespoons

1. Heat the oven to 400°F. Line 1 rimmed baking sheet with a nonstick liner.

2. Set aside 1 tablespoon of the jam for garnish. Put the remaining jam in a medium bowl and stir until well blended and smooth. Add the peaches and gently toss until they are evenly covered with the jam.

3. Carefully unfold or unroll the pie dough, and transfer to the prepared baking sheet. Spoon the peaches and jam into the center of the pastry, mounding slightly, leaving about a 2-inch border. Fold the edges over the filling, pleating and pinching the pastry as you go, leaving the center uncovered. Be careful not to pierce the dough or the jam will leak out during baking. Brush the dough and the inside of the pleats with water and press lightly on the pleats to seal. Sprinkle the sugar over the crust.

4. Bake until the pastry is golden brown and the juices are bubbling, about 45 minutes. Set on a rack to cool slightly, about 10 minutes. Just before serving, spoon the reserved jam over the fruit filling.

Switch-Ins

In place of the seedless raspberry jam, switch in one of the following:
• seedless strawberry jam, or apricot jam, or currant jelly, ½ cup

In place of the peaches, switch in one of the following:
• ripe nectarines, 3 (1 pound total), cut into 1-inch pieces
• ripe plums, 5 (1 pound total), cut into 1-inch pieces

In place of the turbinado sugar, switch in one of the following:
• Sugar in the Raw® or granulated sugar, 2 tablespoons

Gussy It Up

• Drizzle Vanilla or Citrus Glaze (page 180) over the baked and cooled galette.
• Serve with one or more of the following: a scoop of ice cream, Classic Sweetened Whipped Cream (page 180) or one of the caramel sauces (page 179).

Mango and Milk Chocolate Mousse Tartlets

SERVES 4

mango
medium, ripe,
1 (12 ounces), halved and
pitted

**frozen puff pastry
shells**
4

heavy cream
1¼ cups

milk chocolate
6 ounces, chopped (1 cup)

1. Heat the oven to 425°F. Line 1 large cookie sheet with a nonstick liner.

2. Cut the flesh of each mango half into ½-inch crosshatch without piercing the skin. Push up from the skin side and cut away the mango from the skin. Cover and refrigerate until ready to serve.

3. Arrange the frozen shells 3 inches apart on the prepared sheet. Bake until puffed and golden brown, about 20 minutes. Set on a rack to cool slightly. Using a knife, cut and lift off the "hats" and set the shells aside. Scoop out and discard any undercooked dough from inside each shell.

4. Put the cream and chocolate in a medium heatproof bowl and cook in the microwave or over simmering water until the chocolate is melted. Whisk until smooth and blended. Refrigerate, stirring occasionally, until chilled, about 45 minutes. With an electric mixer, beat until medium-firm peaks form when the beaters are lifted, about 1 minute. Don't overbeat or the mousse will be grainy.

5. To serve, arrange the baked shells on small plates, fill with the mousse, and top with mango pieces and pastry "hats." Serve immediately.

Switch-Ins
In place of the mango, switch in one of the following:
• raspberries, ½ pint (6 ounces)
• strawberries, 1 pint (½ pound), hulled and halved or quartered

In place of the puff pastry shells, switch in the following:
• frozen ready-to-fill dessert shells, 4, thawed

In place of the milk chocolate, switch in the following:
• white, bittersweet, or semisweet chocolate, 4 ounces, chopped

Gussy It Up
Drizzle the prepared tartlets with Killer Chocolate Sauce (page 179).

Individual Blackberry Napoleons

SERVES 4

frozen phyllo dough
8 sheets (9 x 13 inches), thawed

granulated sugar
¼ cup

blackberries
1 pint (12 ounces), rinsed and dried

lemon curd
¾ cup

1. Heat the oven to 375°F. Line 2 large cookie sheets with nonstick liners.

2. Arrange 1 sheet of phyllo on the counter, keeping the remaining sheets covered with plastic wrap. Lightly spray the dough with cooking spray and sprinkle with about 1 teaspoon of the sugar. Repeat layering with 3 more dough sheets for a total of 4 layers. Using a sharp knife, trim the layered sheets to $7^{1}/_{2}$ x $11^{3}/_{4}$ inches. Cut into 4 equal squares. Arrange the squares about 1 inch apart on one of the prepared cookie sheets. Repeat with the remaining phyllo and sugar and the other cookie sheet.

3. Bake until golden brown, about 7 minutes. Set on racks to cool completely. Use immediately or cover and store at room temperature until ready to serve or for up to 1 day.

4. To serve, have ready 4 small plates. Set aside the prettiest four phyllo squares and a few blackberries. Divide the remaining berries into 4 equal piles. Arrange the remaining phyllo squares on plates. Carefully spread 2 tablespoons of the curd over each square and top with 1 pile of blackberries. Position the reserved phyllo squares on top of the stacks and garnish with the remaining curd and blackberries.

Switch-Ins
In place of the blackberries, switch in one of the following:
• raspberries, 1 pint (12 ounces)
• blueberries, 1 pint (12 ounces)

In place of the lemon curd, switch in one of the following:
• orange curd, ¾ cup
• grapefruit curd, ¾ cup

Gussy It Up
Stir the following into the sugar:
• pistachios or pecans, finely ground, 2 tablespoons

Toasted Walnut–Apple Butter Tartlets

SERVES 6

walnuts
coarsely chopped,
½ cup

granulated sugar
1 tablespoon

premade pie dough
1 sheet, thawed

apple butter
1¼ cups

1. Heat the oven to 400°F. Lightly grease 6 muffin cups.

2. Put the walnuts and sugar in a small bowl and stir until blended. Set aside.

3. Carefully unfold or unroll the pie dough onto a work surface. Using a 3½-inch round cookie cutter, cut out 6 rounds. Using your fingers, line the prepared muffin cups with the pastry rounds, pressing into the bottoms and up the sides of the cups. Spoon the apple butter evenly into each cup (about 3 tablespoons per cup).

4. Bake for 15 minutes. Scatter the reserved nut-sugar mixture evenly over the filling, then continue baking until the pastry is golden brown and the filling is bubbling, about another 15 minutes. Set on a rack to cool slightly, about 10 minutes, before serving.

Switch-Ins
In place of the walnuts, switch in the following:
• pecans, coarsely chopped, ½ cup

In place of the apple butter, switch in one of the following:
• pear butter, 1¼ cups
• peach butter, 1¼ cups

Gussy It Up
Serve the tarts with a scoop of ice cream, Classic Sweetened Whipped Cream (page 180), one of the caramel sauces (page 179), Easy Butterscotch Sauce (pages 178–179), Boozy Hard Sauce (page 178), or Vanilla or Citrus Glaze (page 180).

Almond Cream–Fig Tartlets

SERVES 6

premade pie dough
1 sheet, thawed

almond paste
firmly packed,
⅓ cup (3½ ounces),
cut into pieces

yolk from large egg
1

figs
small, firm-ripe,
6 (4 ounces each),
rinsed and trimmed

1. Heat the oven to 400°F. Lightly grease 6 muffin cups.

2. Carefully unfold or unroll the pie dough. Using a 3½-inch round cookie cutter, cut out 6 rounds. Using your fingers, line the prepared muffin cups with the pastry rounds, pressing into the bottoms and up the sides of the cups.

3. Put the almond paste in a food processor. Process until fine crumbs form, about 30 seconds. Add the egg yolk and ¼ cup water. Process until well blended and smooth. Spoon the almond cream evenly into each cup.

4. Cut the figs in half lengthwise. Arrange two halves, cut side up, evenly into each cup and press gently into the almond cream.

5. Bake until the filling is puffed and golden brown and the fruit is bubbling, 25 to 28 minutes. Set on a rack to cool slightly, about 10 minutes, before serving.

Switch-Ins
In place of the figs, switch in one of the following:
• small ripe apricots, 3, halved and pitted
• cherries, 12, halved and pitted

Gussy It Up
Top each tartlet with a few sliced almonds before baking as directed.

Fresh Strawberry Pie

SERVES 6 TO 8

strawberries
2 quarts (2 pounds),
rinsed, dried, and hulled,
divided

gelatin
unflavored powder,
1 envelope

**confectioners'
sugar**
¾ cup + more for dusting

**chocolate cookie
pie crust**
1 (6 ounces)

1. Make room in the refrigerator for the pie crust.

2. Cut half of the strawberries (1 quart/1 pound) into halves and put in a blender (but don't process yet). Cut the remaining strawberries lengthwise into halves, then slice; cover and refrigerate.

3. Pour 3 tablespoons water into a small bowl or ramekin and sprinkle the gelatin on top. Let sit until the gelatin is moist and plump, about 3 minutes. Microwave until the gelatin is dissolved and the liquid is clear, 30 to 90 seconds.

4. Put the confectioners' sugar in the blender with the strawberries and process until smooth, about 1 minute. Add the dissolved gelatin and process until well blended, about 5 seconds. Pour into the prepared pie crust, cover loosely, and refrigerate until firm, about 2 hours.

5. Arrange the remaining strawberries on top of the chilled filling. Serve immediately or cover with plastic wrap and refrigerate for up to 1 day. Just before serving, lightly dust the berries with extra confectioners' sugar, if desired.

Switch-Ins
In place of the chocolate cookie pie crust, switch in one of the following:
• graham cracker pie crust, 1 (6 ounces)
• shortbread cookie pie crust, 1 (6 ounces)
• gingersnap cookie pie crust, 1 (6 ounces)

Gussy It Up
• Serve with one of the whipped creams (page 180) and Killer Chocolate Sauce (page 179).
• Drizzle with Chocolate Drizzle (page 178) or Citrus Glaze (page 180).

Caramel Nut Tart

SERVES 6 TO 8

**premade
pie dough**
1 sheet, thawed

caramels
29 small squares
(8 ounces), unwrapped

heavy cream
3 tablespoons

**unsalted
mixed nuts**
roughly chopped,
1½ cups (6 ounces),
toasted

1. Carefully unfold or unroll the pie dough. Transfer the dough to a 9½-inch tart pan with a removable bottom. Using your fingers, press the dough into the bottom and up the sides of the pan. Using your thumb, remove any excess dough by pressing it against the rim of the pan. Slide the lined tart pan into the freezer to chill while the oven heats.

2. Heat the oven to 425°F. Blind-bake the crust until golden brown (see page 182 for more info). Set on a rack to cool while the filling is prepared.

3. Put the caramels and heavy cream in a medium heatproof bowl and cook in the microwave or over simmering water until the caramels are melted and the mixture is very hot. Whisk until smooth and blended. Add the toasted nuts and stir until blended. If the mixture is too sticky, cook a minute or two until the caramel is pourable. Scrape into the baked tart crust and spread evenly. Chill until firm, about 30 minutes, or cover and refrigerate for up to 1 day. Serve slightly chilled.

Switch-Ins

In place of the premade pie dough, switch in the following:
• frozen ready-to-fill dessert shells, 6, thawed (portion the caramel mixture evenly into the shells)

In place of the unsalted mixed nuts, switch in the following:
• any combination or single variety of unsalted nuts, roughly chopped, 1½ cups, toasted

Gussy It Up
• Drizzle the tart with Chocolate Drizzle (page 178).
• Serve with Classic Sweetened Whipped Cream (page 180), or vanilla ice cream.

Chunky Apple Brown Betty

SERVES 6

large apples
4 (2 pounds total)

English muffins
3, split

cinnamon sugar
¾ cup

unsalted butter
4 tablespoons, melted

1. Heat the oven to 375°F. Lightly grease an 8-inch-square baking dish.

2. Peel, core, and cut the apples into ½-inch slices.

3. Tear the muffin halves into pieces and put in a food processor. Process until fine crumbs form, about 30 seconds. You should have 2½ cups crumbs. Put the crumbs and cinnamon sugar in a medium bowl and stir until blended. Drizzle the melted butter over the crumbs and toss until well blended.

4. Put about one-third of the breadcrumbs in the prepared pan and spread evenly. Layer the apple slices on top of the crumbs. Drizzle with 3 table-spoons water. Scatter the remaining crumbs evenly over the apples.

5. Bake until the crumbs are well browned and the apples are tender, about 45 minutes. If the crumbs begin to burn, cover loosely with foil. Serve warm.

Switch-Ins
In place of the apples, switch in one of the following:
• ripe pears, 6 (2 pounds total)
• firm-ripe peaches, 6 (2 pounds total)

In place of the English muffins, switch in the following:
• white bread, 4 to 5 slices (to make 2½ cups crumbs)

Gussy It Up
• Add 1 cup chopped pecans or walnuts to the breadcrumb mixture and proceed as directed.
• Serve with Classic Sweetened Whipped Cream (page 180), Boozy Hard Sauce (page 178), crème fraîche, or vanilla ice cream.

Tech Talk
Make your own cinnamon sugar: Mix ¾ cup granulated sugar with 2 table-spoons ground cinnamon.

Raspberry–White Chocolate Tart

SERVES 8

gingersnap cookie pie crust
1 (6 ounces)

white chocolate
9 ounces, chopped and melted, divided

heavy cream
¾ cup

raspberries
1 pint (12 ounces), rinsed and dried

1. Have ready a 9½-inch tart pan with removable bottom. Crumble the cookie pie crust into a medium bowl and microwave until warm, about 1½ minutes. Stir until completely broken up. Dump the warm crumbs into the tart pan and press evenly onto the bottom and up the sides of the pan. Refrigerate until chilled, about 20 minutes.

2. Spoon 2 tablespoons of the melted white chocolate into one corner of a small zip-top plastic bag and set aside. Put the remaining chocolate and heavy cream in a medium bowl. Whisk until smooth and blended. Refrigerate, if needed, until chilled, about 20 minutes.

3. Beat the chocolate–cream mixture using an electric mixer until fluffy and firm, about 1 minute. Don't overbeat or the cream will be grainy.

4. Spoon the mixture into the tart crust and spread evenly. Arrange the raspberries on top of the filling. Snip the corner of the plastic bag and drizzle melted white chocolate over the top. Serve immediately (the filling will be soft) or cover with plastic wrap and refrigerate for 30 minutes or up to 1 day. Just before serving, remove the outer ring and carefully slide the tart, still on the pan bottom, onto a flat serving plate. Warm the chocolate in a zip-top bag, snip the corner of the bag, and drizzle over the top of the tart.

Tech Talk
To press the crumbs evenly into the bottom of the tart pan, cover the crumbs with a piece of plastic wrap and, using a straight-sided, flat-bottomed mug, press the crumbs evenly onto the bottom and sides of the pan.

Switch-Ins
In place of the gingersnap cookie pie crust, switch in one of the following:
• graham cracker pie crust, 1 (6 ounces)
• shortbread cookie pie crust, 1 (6 ounces)
• chocolate cookie pie crust, 1 (6 ounces)

In place of the tart pan, switch in one of the following:
• prepared pie crust, any flavor, 1

In place of the raspberries, switch in the following:
• mixed berries, 2⅔ cups

Honey Cranberry Tartlets

SERVES 4

whole cranberries
fresh or frozen,
¾ cup

honey
½ cup + 2 tablespoons,
divided

**frozen puff pastry
shells**
4

mascarpone
½ cup

1. Heat the oven to 425°F. Line 1 large cookie sheet with a nonstick liner.

2. Pile the cranberries, ½ cup of the honey, and ¼ cup water into a small saucepan. Cook over medium heat until boiling. Reduce the heat to medium low and simmer, stirring frequently, until very thick and jam-like, 3 to 7 minutes. You'll have about ⅔ cup compote. Set aside to cool slightly or cover and refrigerate for up to 3 days before reheating and serving.

3. Arrange the frozen tart shells about 3 inches apart on the prepared cookie sheet. Bake until puffed and deep golden brown, about 20 minutes. Set on a rack to cool slightly, about 5 minutes. Using a small knife, carefully cut and lift off the "hats" and set the shells aside. Scoop out and discard any undercooked dough from inside each shell. Set the shells aside.

4. Put the mascarpone and the remaining 2 tablespoons honey in a small bowl and stir until well blended and smooth.

5. To serve, gently reheat the cranberry compote, if necessary, until warm. Arrange the warm, baked shells on small plates and spoon the mascarpone evenly into the shells, then top with 1 or 2 tablespoons of the warm compote. Arrange the reserved "hats" on the compote and serve immediately.

Switch-Ins
In place of the honey, switch in the following:
• pure maple syrup, ⅔ cup (don't use water)

In place of the puff pastry shells, switch in the following:
• frozen ready-to-fill dessert shells, 4, thawed

Gussy It Up
Sprinkle each tartlet with chopped pistachios and serve with Citrus Glaze (page 180).

Concord Grape "Pot Pies"

SERVES 4

cornstarch
2 tablespoons

Concord grapes
3 cups (1¼ pounds with stems)

granulated sugar
1 cup, divided

frozen phyllo dough
16 sheets (9 x 13 inches), thawed

1. Put a small, foil-lined baking sheet in the oven; heat the oven to 375°F. Lightly grease four 6-ounce ramekins and set aside. Put the cornstarch and 2 tablespoons water in a ramekin and stir until smooth. Set aside.

2. Pinch the grapes, slipping the skins from the stem end; set aside. Put the grapes and ¾ cup sugar in a medium saucepan. Cook, stirring over medium-low heat until the sugar is dissolved and the fruit bursts when pressed against the pan, about 5 minutes. Taste and add sugar, if needed.

3. Strain the mixture through a fine-mesh sieve into a medium bowl, pressing on the solids, to yield 1¼ cups. Discard the solids. Put the purée back in the pan and add the skins. Cook over medium-low heat, stirring and pressing the skins, until just boiling. Whisk in the cornstarch mixture until just boiling. Pour into the ramekins; set aside.

4. Arrange 1 sheet of phyllo on the counter; keep the remaining sheets covered with plastic. Lightly spray the dough with cooking spray and sprinkle with ¾ teaspoon of the remaining sugar. Add another sheet and repeat layering with sugar and the remaining sheets for a total of 16 layers. Using a sharp knife and an inverted ramekin as a guide, cut the layered dough into 4 rounds. Cut two 1-inch long slits in an X in the center of each round. Carefully arrange the phyllo rounds on top of the warm grape filling in the ramekins and sprinkle any remaining sugar on top.

5. Arrange on the baking sheet. Bake until the pastry is browned and the filling is bubbling, 20 to 25 minutes. Let cool for 10 minutes; serve warm.

Switch-Ins
In place of the granulated sugar, switch in one of the following:
• granulated maple sugar, ⅔ cup
• brown sugar, ⅔ cup, firmly packed

Ice Cream Puffs

MAKES 12 PUFFS; SERVES 4 TO 6

large eggs
2 whole + 1 yolk, divided

unsalted butter
3 tablespoons, cut into
6 pieces

all-purpose flour
½ cup

**chunky chocolate
fudge swirl ice
cream**
1 pint

1. Heat the oven to 425°F. Line 1 large cookie sheet with a nonstick liner.

2. Put the egg yolk and 1 tablespoon water in a small bowl or ramekin and mix with a fork until blended. Set aside.

3. Put the butter, ½ cup water, and ¼ teaspoon salt in a medium saucepan. Bring to a boil over high heat. As soon as it's boiling, slide the pan from the heat and immediately add all the flour. Using a spoon, stir quickly until the dough is smooth and thick. Cook over low heat, stirring constantly, until the dough is shiny, about 1 minute.

4. Slide the pan from the heat and add 1 egg, beating until it's well blended and the dough is smooth. Add the remaining egg and beat until the dough is smooth and soft. The dough should fall from the spoon by the count of three.

5. With a mini ice cream scoop, drop the dough in 1¼-inch mounds about 1½ inches apart onto the prepared cookie sheet. Brush the tops with the reserved whisked egg yolk. Bake until puffed and deep golden brown, about 27 minutes. Set on a rack, pierce the side of each puff with the tip of a knife, and let cool completely. Use immediately or cover and store at room temperature for up to 1 day or freeze for up to 1 month.

6. To serve, cut each puff in half crosswise and fill generously with a scoop of hard ice cream, then replace the puff lids. Arrange in small shallow bowls or rimmed plates and serve immediately.

Switch-Ins
In place of the chocolate fudge swirl ice cream, switch in any flavor you like.

Gussy It Up
Serve with Killer Chocolate Sauce (page 179), Double Whole Berry Sauce (page 178), Easy Butterscotch Sauce (pages 178–179), or one of the caramel sauces (page 179).

Classic Pear Ginger Turnovers

SERVES 4

pear
large, ripe,
1 (8 ounces)

brown sugar
4 tablespoons, firmly
packed, divided

fresh ginger
minced,
¾ teaspoon

**frozen puff pastry
sheet**
1 (about 9 ounces),
thawed

1. Heat the oven to 400°F. Line 1 large cookie sheet with a nonstick liner.

2. Peel, core, and coarsely chop the pear. Put the pears, 3 tablespoons of the brown sugar, and the ginger in a small bowl and toss until blended.

3. Arrange a large piece of plastic wrap on the counter and lightly coat with cooking spray. Unfold the puff pastry sheet on the plastic wrap. Lightly spray the top of the pastry and cover with another piece of plastic wrap. Using a rolling pin, roll out the puff pastry sheet into an 11¾-inch square. Using a sharp knife, trim the pastry to about an 11½-inch square, then cut into 4 smaller squares.

4. Put an equal amount of pear filling diagonally along the center of each square. Brush the edges of the dough with water. Fold half of the dough over the filling to form a triangle. Using the tines of a fork, press the edges to seal tightly.

5. Arrange the turnovers on the prepared cookie sheet about 3 inches apart. Lightly spray the tops with cooking spray and sprinkle evenly with the remaining brown sugar. Bake until the pastry is puffed and browned, about 28 minutes. Serve warm.

Switch-Ins
In place of the pear, switch in the following:
• small, ripe prune plums, 8 ounces, pitted and chopped

In place of the fresh ginger, switch in one of the following:
• crystallized ginger, finely chopped, 1½ tablespoons
• ground cinnamon, ½ teaspoon

Gussy It Up
• Drizzle the baked and cooled turnovers with Vanilla or Citrus Glaze (page 180).
• Serve warm with a scoop or two of vanilla or maple walnut ice cream.

Grilled Pineapple Maple Tart

SERVES 4

frozen puff pastry sheet
1 (about 9 ounces), thawed

pineapple
large, ripe, 1 (8 ounces)

mascarpone
¾ cup

pure maple syrup
5 tablespoons, divided

1. Arrange a large piece of plastic wrap on the counter and lightly coat with cooking spray. Unfold the puff pastry sheet on the plastic wrap. Lightly spray the top of the pastry and cover with another piece of plastic wrap. Using a rolling pin, roll out the puff pastry sheet into a 10-inch square and prick all over using the tines of a fork. Transfer the dough to a 9½-inch tart pan with a removable bottom. Using your fingers, press the dough into the bottom and up the sides of the pan. Using your thumb, remove any excess dough by pressing it against the top edge of the pan. Slide the lined tart pan into the freezer while the oven heats.

2. Heat the oven to 425°F. Blind-bake the crust until golden brown (see page 182 for more info). Set on a rack to cool completely.

3. Using a serrated knife, remove the top and a thin slice of the base from the pineapple. Stand the pineapple on one end and cut away all the skin and brown spots, then cut into quarters lengthwise. Turn the pineapple quarters on a flat side and cut out the core to make 4 long spears.

4. Just before serving, heat the grill to medium. Put the mascarpone and 4 tablespoons of the maple syrup in a small bowl and mix until well blended. Scrape into the baked and cooled tart shell and spread evenly. Put the pineapple spears on the hot grill. Cook, turning, until caramelized on each side, about 4 minutes. Cut the spears into ¼-inch-thick slices. Arrange the slices on top of the cream and drizzle with the remaining 1 tablespoon maple syrup. Serve while the pineapple is warm.

Switch-Ins
In place of the whole pineapple, switch in the following:
• fresh peeled, cored pineapple, store bought, 1

Gussy It Up
Sprinkle with toasted, chopped pistachios or macadamia nuts.

Caramelized Plum Tartlets

SERVES 4

**frozen puff pastry
shells**
4

plums
medium, ripe,
3 (1 pound), rinsed
and dried

granulated sugar
⅓ cup

crème fraîche
1 cup

1. Heat the oven to 425°F. Line 1 large cookie sheet with a nonstick liner.

2. Arrange the frozen tart shells about 3 inches apart on the prepared cookie sheet. Bake until puffed and deep golden brown, about 20 minutes. Set on a rack to cool slightly, about 5 minutes. Using a small knife, carefully cut and lift off the "hats" and set aside. Scoop out and discard any undercooked dough from inside each shell. Set aside.

3. Cut each plum into 6 wedges. Put the sugar, a pinch of salt, and 1 tablespoon water into a medium skillet. Cook over medium heat, swirling the pan frequently, until the caramel is golden amber, about 3 minutes. Carefully add the plums, a cut side down, in an even layer to the pan. Continue cooking, gently shaking the pan, until the plums are caramelized on the bottom, about 3 minutes. Turn the plums and cook until caramelized, about 3 minutes. Slide the skillet from the heat and set aside.

4. To serve, arrange the baked shells on small plates. Fill with some crème fraîche, top with the warm plums and caramel sauce and remaining crème fraîche.

Switch-Ins
In place of the puff pastry shells, switch in the following:
• frozen ready-to-fill dessert shells, 4, thawed

In place of the plums, switch in one of the following:
• ripe nectarines, 3 (1 pound)
• ripe pluots, 3 (1 pound)
• ripe peaches, 3 (1 pound)

In place of the crème fraîche, switch in the following:
• sour cream, ¾ cup

Gussy It Up
Add the following to the caramel along with the plums:
• fresh ginger, finely chopped, 1 teaspoon

Peach Cobbler with Phyllo Topping

SERVES 6

cinnamon sugar
¼ cup + 1½ tablespoons

frozen phyllo dough
8 sheets (9 x 13 inches), thawed

peaches
ripe, 6 (2 pounds), rinsed and dried

all-purpose flour
2 tablespoons

1. Have ready 1½ tablespoons of the cinnamon sugar (see Tech Talk, page 165). Arrange 1 sheet of phyllo on the counter, keeping the remaining sheets covered with plastic wrap. Lightly spray the dough with cooking spray and sprinkle with about ½ teaspoon of the cinnamon sugar. Repeat layering with the remaining sheets and sugar for a total of 8 layers.

2. Starting at one short side, roll up the sheets jellyroll style. Using a sharp knife, cut the roll into 1-inch slices. Put the pieces in a medium bowl and gently toss with your fingers until the strips are separated and loose. Set aside, tossing occasionally, while you make the filling. The strips will dry out slightly so that they hold their shape a bit better.

3. Heat the oven to 400°F. Have ready an 8-cup baking dish.

4. Cut the peaches into quarters. Pile the peaches, the remaining ¼ cup cinnamon sugar, and the flour in the baking dish. Toss until well blended and spread evenly. Gently toss the strips again and loosely spread them over the fruit. Bake until the phyllo is golden brown and the peaches are tender, about 40 minutes. Check the cobbler after 15 minutes; if the phyllo is darkening, cover loosely with foil. Set on rack and let cool for at least 15 minutes before serving.

Switch-Ins
In place of the cinnamon sugar, switch in the following:
• granulated sugar, ⅓ cup + 1½ tablespoons

In place of the peaches, switch in one of the following:
• plums, 8 (2 pounds), cut into quarters
• apricots, 8 (2 pounds) cut into eighths
• nectarines, 6 (2 pounds), cut into eighths

Gussy It Up
Serve with a scoop of ice cream or a dollop of Classic Sweetened Whipped Cream (page 180).

add-ons

Although the recipes in this book are sensational on their own, you'll probably have an occasion, time permitting, when you'll want to dress up a dessert—what I call "gussying up"—by pairing it with an easy-to-prepare sauce, glaze, or whipped topping. The recipes in this book are simple and easy, but that doesn't mean they lack flavor, complexity, and sophistication, so the quick and easy add-ons you'll find here won't overpower any of the desserts but rather make them a bit more decadent.

Boozy hard sauce. Combine 4 ounces room-temperature unsalted butter and 1 cup confectioners' sugar in a medium bowl. Beat with an electric mixer on low speed until the ingredients are blended. Add 1 tablespoon brandy or dark rum **or** ¾ teaspoon pure vanilla extract **or** 1 teaspoon finely grated citrus zest and a pinch of table salt. Increase the speed to medium and beat until smooth and fluffy. Serve immediately or cover and refrigerate for up to 2 weeks. The sauce can be served cold or at room temperature. Makes about ⅔ cup.

Caramelized brittle topping for cheesecakes or custards. Just before serving, sift ½ cup granulated sugar evenly over the top of the cheesecake. Using a small hand-held kitchen torch, pass the flame evenly over the sugar until it melts and caramelizes.

Chocolate drizzle or coating. Put 3 ounces chopped bittersweet or semisweet chocolate and 2 teaspoons vegetable shortening or neutral-flavored vegetable oil in a small heatproof bowl and cook in the microwave or over simmering water until the chocolate is melted. Whisk until smooth and blended. Dip or drizzle cookies, tarts, or fruit with chocolate and set aside until the chocolate is set or, for faster setting, refrigerate for about 15 minutes. Leftover chocolate can be covered and refrigerated for up to 5 days before reheating and using. Makes about ¼ cup.

Decorative stencil topping. Position strips of heavy-duty paper decoratively on the top of the cooled dessert. Put 2 to 4 tablespoons confectioners' sugar or unsweetened cocoa powder in a small sieve and sift evenly and generously over the dessert, then carefully remove the strips.

Double whole berry sauce. Rinse, dry, and hull 1 quart of strawberries and cut in half, if very large. Put the berries and ½ cup granulated sugar in a medium saucepan. Cook, stirring frequently, over medium-low heat, until the sugar is dissolved and the strawberries are juicy and tender. Slide the pan from the heat and stir in ½ pint raspberries and ½ teaspoon finely grated lemon or orange zest. Cool slightly or cover and refrigerate for up to 2 days until ready to serve. The sauce can be served warm or cold. Makes about 1½ cups.

Easy butterscotch sauce. Put 1 cup firmly packed brown sugar, 8 tablespoons unsalted butter, and 1 tablespoon light corn syrup in a medium saucepan. Cook over medium heat, stirring, until the sugar is dissolved and the mixture is boiling. Slide the pan from the heat and carefully add ⅓ cup heavy cream, ½ teaspoon pure vanilla extract, and a pinch of table salt. Cook, whisking, over medium heat until smooth and well blended. Serve warm or cover and refrigerate for up to 2 weeks before reheating and serving. Makes about 1⅓ cups.

Easy, creamy caramel sauce. Put 22 small caramels, unwrapped, and ¼ cup heavy cream in a medium heatproof bowl and cook in the microwave or over simmering water until the caramels are melted and the mixture is very hot. Whisk until smooth and blended. Serve hot or warm or cover and refrigerate for up to 5 days before reheating and serving. Makes about ¾ cup.

Espresso or vanilla reduced cream sauce. Put 1½ cups heavy cream in a medium saucepan and bring to a boil. Reduce the heat and simmer vigorously until the cream is thick enough to coat the back of a spoon (you'll have about 1 cup), about 10 minutes. Slide the pan from the heat, add 1 to 2 tablespoons granulated sugar and whisk until dissolved. Add ½ teaspoon instant espresso or coffee powder **or** ½ teaspoon pure vanilla extract. Taste and add more sugar or flavoring. Serve warm or cover the surface with plastic wrap and refrigerate for up to 3 days until ready to serve. The sauce can be served warm or cold. Makes about 1 cup.

"From scratch" caramel sauce. Put 1 cup granulated sugar, ¼ cup water, and 1 tablespoon light corn syrup in a medium saucepan. Cook over medium heat, stirring, until the sugar is dissolved. Increase the heat to high and cook, swirling the pan over the heat but not stirring, until the syrup

is deep amber. Slide the pan from the heat and carefully add ½ cup heavy cream, 4 tablespoons unsalted butter, and a pinch of table salt. Cook, whisking, over medium heat until smooth and well blended. Serve warm or cover and refrigerate for up to 2 weeks before reheating and serving. Makes about 1¼ cups.

Glossy fresh fruit glaze. Put ¼ cup seedless jam (currant, apple, strawberry, apricot) and 2 tablespoons water or flavored liqueur in a small heatproof bowl. Microwave until hot, about 1 to 2 minutes, and stir until blended and smooth. Using a small pastry brush, lightly dab the warm glaze over the fruit. Makes about ⅓ cup.

Killer chocolate sauce. Put 6 ounces chopped bittersweet or semisweet chocolate, 4 ounces unsalted butter, and 2 tablespoons light corn syrup in a small heatproof bowl and cook in the microwave or over simmering water until the chocolate and butter are melted. Whisk until smooth and blended. Serve warm or at room temperature. Leftover sauce can be covered and refrigerated for up to 5 days before reheating and serving. Makes about 1 cup.

Ruby red cranberry sauce. Put 1 cup fresh or frozen cranberries, ¾ cup cranberry juice cocktail, and ¾ cup granulated sugar in a small saucepan. Bring to a boil, stirring occasionally, over medium-high heat. Reduce the heat to medium low and simmer, stirring occasionally, until the berries are very soft, about 6 minutes. Strain the mixture through a fine-mesh sieve into a small bowl, pressing firmly on the solids. Discard the solids and serve immediately or cover and refrigerate for up to 2 weeks. The sauce can be served cold or warm. Makes about 1¼ cups.

Vanilla or citrus glaze. Put 1 cup confectioners' sugar and ¼ cup heavy cream in a small bowl and stir until well blended and glossy. Stir in ¼ teaspoon pure vanilla extract **or** 1 teaspoon finely grated orange, lemon, or lime zest. If the glaze is too thick, add a drop more of heavy cream; if it's too thin, add a bit more confectioners' sugar. Makes about ½ cup.

WHIPPED CREAMS

Classic sweetened whipped cream. Put ¾ cup heavy cream, 2 tablespoons granulated or light brown sugar, ½ teaspoon pure vanilla extract, and a pinch of table salt in a medium bowl. Beat with an electric mixer on medium-high speed until medium-firm peaks form when the beaters are lifted (don't forget to stop the mixer first!). Serve immediately or cover and refrigerate for up to 1 hour before serving. Makes about 1½ cups.

Chocolate whipped cream. Put 3 tablespoons Dutch-processed cocoa powder, ½ cup confectioners' sugar, ¼ teaspoon pure vanilla extract, and a pinch of table salt in a medium bowl. Add ¼ cup heavy cream and beat with an electric mixer on low speed until well blended, about 20 seconds. Add ¾ cup heavy cream and beat on medium-high speed until medium-firm peaks form when the beaters are lifted (don't forget to stop the mixer first!). Serve immediately or cover and refrigerate for up to 1 hour before serving. Makes about 1⅔ cups.

Whipped mascarpone cream. Put ½ cup mascarpone, ½ cup heavy cream, 2 tablespoons light brown or granulated sugar, and ½ teaspoon pure vanilla extract in a medium bowl. Beat with an electric mixer on low speed until the ingredients are blended. Increase the speed to medium high and beat until medium-firm peaks form when the beaters are lifted (don't forget to stop the mixer first!). Serve immediately or cover and refrigerate for up to 6 hours before serving. Makes about 1½ cups.

Whipped cream variations. Fold in ¼ cup chopped toffee bits **or** ¼ cup toasted and chopped nuts **or** ¼ cup finely chopped chocolate (or mini chips) **or** 3 tablespoons finely chopped crystallized ginger **or** 1 tablespoon flavored liqueur **or** 1 tablespoon finely grated orange zest **or** 1½ teaspoons finely grated lemon or lime zest into the Classic Sweetened, Chocolate, or Mascarpone Whipped Cream.

Fruit-flavored whipped cream. Fold ¾ to 1 cup unsweetened fresh fruit purée (strawberry, apricot, mango, papaya, blueberry) into the Classic Sweetened or Mascarpone Whipped Cream. Makes about 2 cups.

Fruit preserve whipped cream. Put 1 cup heavy cream, 3 tablespoons seedless jam or preserve (marmalade, apricot, raspberry), and 2 tablespoons confectioners' sugar in a medium bowl. Beat with an electric mixer on low speed until the ingredients are blended. Increase the speed to medium high and beat until medium-firm peaks form when the beaters are lifted (don't forget to stop the mixer first!). Serve immediately. Makes about 1¾ cups.

essentials

Insider knowledge is a bad thing in the finance world but a great thing in the dessert biz! Here you'll find tips, techniques, and tricks that I've picked up throughout my baking career. Along with some brief equipment, ingredient, and technique explanations, I've included a few "from scratch" recipes that you can "switch in" for their store-bought counterparts. Consider this section your arsenal and resource—turn to it when you have ingredient questions, need some more info on a subject, or want to double-check a method or technique.

INGREDIENTS

Aged balsamic vinegar. The longer balsamic vinegar is aged, the darker, thicker, and sweeter its taste.

Cocoa powder. Made from roasted cocoa beans pulverized into a paste and then dried and ground, this fine powder is unsweetened. Not to be confused with sweetened cocoa mix, it is available in natural or Dutch processed. Dutch-processed cocoa is treated with an alkaline to neutralize the acid, giving it a smoother taste. The varieties aren't always interchangeable, so it's best to use what's called for in the recipe. You can use either type in these recipes. If your cocoa is lumpy, sift before measuring.

Crystallized ginger. Also known as candied ginger. Peeled and sliced fresh ginger is cooked in dense sugar syrup until tender and then coated with granulated sugar. It has a sweet-spicy taste and a soft, candy-like texture. Stored in an airtight container in the pantry, it will stay moist for up to 3 months.

Dulce de leche. This very thick, sweet milk sauce is similar in taste to caramel. Widely available in cans and jars, it's also easy to make at home. Pour 1 can (14 or 14½ ounces) sweetened condensed milk (not evaporated) into a medium saucepan. Cook, stirring frequently, over low heat until golden brown, creamy, and very thick, about 22 minutes. Stir in ¼ teaspoon pure vanilla extract and a pinch of table salt. Let cool completely before using or cover and refrigerate for up to 1 week.

Fresh ginger. Also known as ginger root. Select pieces that are hard and not shriveled or dry looking. Before grating, slicing, or chopping, remove the thin gray-brown peel by running the edge of a spoon in short, firm strokes over the ginger until the peel is scraped off. For finely grated ginger, I like to use a Microplane grater, but a small porcelain ginger grater works well, too.

Gelatin. Unflavored powdered gelatin is used to thicken many chilled desserts. Soften the powder in liquid, as directed, until it's plump and moist then heat gently in a microwave or over simmering water until the liquid is clear and no granules remain. Avoid boiling, as that can affect its thickening power.

Half-and-half. Half-and-half is made with half milk and half heavy cream. If you have both heavy cream and milk in the fridge, feel free to "switch in" equal parts of each for the amount of half-and-half called for in a recipe. Do not, however, substitute for heavy cream—it can't be whipped.

Homemade cookie crust. In a small bowl, mix 1 cup (4½ ounces) cookie crumbs, 2 tablespoons granulated sugar, and 3 tablespoons melted unsalted butter until well blended. Scrape into an ungreased 9½-inch fluted tart pan with a removable bottom or a 9-inch glass pie plate. Cover with a piece of plastic wrap and, using your hands or a flat-bottomed cup, press evenly into the bottom and up the sides of the pan. Bake the crust in a 350°F oven until fragrant, about 12 minutes. Let cool completely before continuing with the recipe.

Ladyfingers. These long, finger-shaped cookies can be crisp or soft and are available in most grocery stores. The recipes in this book call for the soft variety but feel free to experiment with the crisp ones.

Phyllo (or filo). This flour-based, commercially made dough is carefully stretched and pulled until it's so thin that it's practically transparent. Cut into rectangles, the layers or sheets are stacked and rolled together and frozen. Recipes typically use many sheets layered with butter (or other fat) and sometimes sugar, which bake up into crisp, flaky pastries, shells, or toppings. A cautionary word: When working with phyllo, keep dough sheets not in use covered with plastic wrap to prevent them from drying out and becoming brittle.

Sweetened dried coconut. Most grocery stores will sell both shredded and flaked coconut. For these recipes, either variety may be used, as long as it's sweetened.

TECHNIQUES

Beating egg whites. Impeccably clean beaters and a stainless-steel or glass bowl are a must for beating whites—even a touch of grease makes for flat, unbeatable whites. While it's easiest to separate the egg whites when the eggs are cold, they get the most volume when at room temperature. So, separate first and then warm to room temp before beating. Beat slowly at first, until they're foamy, then gradually increase the speed and proceed as directed in the recipe. Be careful not to overbeat or the whites will be dry and may deflate.

Blind baking. There are two methods.

- **Traditional method:** Line the chilled crust with a large piece of foil and fill with pie weights, dried beans, or uncooked rice. Bake until set, about 20 minutes. Carefully remove the foil and beans (these can both be reused) and continue baking until the crust is golden brown, another 8 to 10 minutes.

- **Pie plate method** (the sides slip down a bit, but this is an easy alternative to the traditional method): Lightly grease the bottom of a 9-inch glass pie plate and place, greased side down, in the chilled crust. Bake until the crust is golden brown, about 25 minutes. Remove the top pie plate.

Brushing with an egg wash. Brushing pastry dough with an egg mixture before baking helps toppings stick and gives a shiny gloss to the finished pastry. In a small bowl or ramekin, whisk 1 egg with 1 tablespoon water, milk, heavy cream, or half-and-half until blended. Use a pastry brush to lightly and evenly coat the dough before adding any toppings.

Chopping dried fruit and crystallized ginger. Stack the fruit or ginger on a cutting board that's secured by placing a damp paper towel under it. To keep the fruit or ginger from sticking to the knife while chopping, lightly coat the knife with oil or spray; repeat as needed.

Crushing cookies. To make crumbled cookies or cookie crumbs, pile the cookies into a food processor and pulse until they reach the desired texture. Or pop them into a heavy-duty zip-top bag, press out all the air, and seal. Using a rolling pin or a small skillet, pound on the cookies until they're the correct consistency.

Cutting a mango. Cut the flesh of each mango half into 1-inch crosshatch without piercing the skin. Push up from the skin side (it will look like a porcupine) and cut away the mango from the skin.

Finely grating citrus zest. Scrub and dry the fruit well. Drag a Microplane zester with small rasps over the rind in short strokes, turning the fruit as necessary to avoid the bitter white pith.

Freezing berries. Arrange rinsed and dried berries in a single layer on a baking sheet or large plate. Freeze until very firm and transfer to freezer bags or containers and keep frozen until ready to use or for up to 6 months.

Getting to know your oven. It's important to know how your oven heats. Oven temps can vary widely, so put a mercury-filled thermometer (the most accurate, in my opinion) in your oven. Check the temp occasionally to be sure it's in sync with the temperature controls. If not, adjust up or down, accordingly. Also, keep an eye out for "hot spots" in your oven—these devilish pockets are hotter than other areas of your oven and can cause overbrowning and overcooking. If you have 'em, simply rotate your pans about halfway through the suggested baking time.

Handling berries. Pick through the berries, discarding any leaves and stems, as well as any bruised or moldy ones. Put the berries in a colander and rinse with cold water. Line a baking sheet with several layers of paper towels or a clean kitchen towel and arrange the berries in an even layer. Cover with more towels and pat dry.

Hulling strawberries. Using a small knife, cut away the stem and white core of rinsed and dried berries. Proceed according to the recipe's directions.

Measuring flour. Proper measuring of all ingredients is important, but measuring flour is of the utmost importance to ensure consistent and accurate baked results. If you use a scale to measure your flour, use this ratio as a reference: 1 cup all-purpose flour weighs 4.5 ounces. If you don't use a scale, use the spoon-and-sweep method: Stir the flour in the container, lightly spoon into the appropriate metal measuring cup—no scooping, packing, or tapping, please— and sweep off the excess with a flat edge (a ruler, the back of a knife, or a spatula handle).

Melting chocolate. Chopped chocolate can be melted in the microwave or on the stovetop. To melt in the microwave, put the chopped chocolate in a heatproof or microwave-safe bowl. Microwave in 30-second bursts (to avoid scorching) until the chocolate is soft and shiny but not completely melted. Stir until smooth. For stovetop melting, use a traditional double boiler (two nesting saucepans) or a saucepan or skillet and a heatproof bowl. Fill the bottom saucepan with water and bring to a simmer. Put the chopped chocolate in a heatproof bowl and set over the simmering water, stirring occasionally, until the chocolate is almost completely melted. Remove from the heat and stir until smooth.

Pitting fruit. Stone tree fruit, like peaches, have a pesky pit in their middle. Use a small knife to cut the fruit in half lengthwise around the pit. Gently turn each half in opposite directions to separate them. If possible, lift the pit out with the tip of the knife and cut as directed. If the fruit halves won't twist or the pit is stubborn, use the knife to cut wedges from the pit and then proceed with the recipe.

Removing citrus zest. Scrub and dry the fruit well. Using a vegetable peeler, shave off long strips of the rind (the colored part of the peel). Cut away the bitter pith (the white part) from the rind with a small, sharp knife. Slice or chop the rind as directed and discard the pith.

Separating eggs. Tap the egg against the rim of a small bowl or ramekin. Working over the bowl, separate the shell into 2 halves, being careful to keep the yolk in one half. Pass the yolk from shell to shell, allowing the white to drop into the bowl. Put the yolk and white in separate mixing bowls. Using the same method, separate any remaining eggs over an empty bowl or ramekin before adding to the mixing bowl to avoid any yolk contamination.

Softening butter. Many recipes call for the butter to be softened to room temperature in order for the batter to mix up thoroughly. This means that the butter shouldn't be too hard or too soft, or worse, melted—it needs to be only soft enough to give slightly when pressed with a finger. This is problematic seeing as how it's kept in the fridge, right? If you haven't been able to plan ahead and have your butter waiting on the counter for you, use the microwave, but use it judiciously. Put the wrapped butter stick in the microwave, and cook in short 5-second bursts, turning and rotating the stick, until the butter passes the finger-press test. If you've gone too far, pop the stick back into the fridge and start again with a fresh one.

Toasting nuts and shredded coconut. Toasting heightens the flavor of nuts and shredded coconut. Heat the oven to 350°F. Spread the nuts or coconut on a baking pan in an even layer. Bake, stirring once or twice, until golden brown and fragrant, about 7 to 12 minutes (depending on size and variety). Let cool completely before using. Store in heavy-duty plastic bags in the freezer.

Unmolding gelatin desserts. Most gelatin desserts can be unmolded up to 1 hour before serving. Have serving plates ready and fill a shallow bowl large enough to fit your mold with very hot water. Working with one ramekin at a time, carefully run a thin knife between the dessert and the inside of the mold. Dip the bottom of the ramekin in the hot water for 15 to 20 seconds. Invert onto a plate and remove the ramekin. If it's stubborn, dip the bottom into hot water and try again.

equivalency charts

liquid/dry measures	
U.S.	Metric
¼ teaspoon	1.25 milliliters
½ teaspoon	2.5 milliliters
1 teaspoon	5 milliliters
1 tablespoon (3 teaspoons)	15 milliliters
1 fluid ounce (2 tablespoons)	30 milliliters
¼ cup	60 milliliters
⅓ cup	80 milliliters
½ cup	120 milliliters
1 cup	240 milliliters
1 pint (2 cups)	480 milliliters
1 quart (4 cups; 32 ounces)	960 milliliters
1 gallon (4 quarts)	3.84 liters
1 ounce (by weight)	28 grams
1 pound	454 grams
2.2 pounds	1 kilogram

oven temperatures		
°F	Gas Mark	°C
250	½	120
275	1	140
300	2	150
325	3	165
350	4	180
375	5	190
400	6	200
425	7	220
450	8	230
475	9	240
500	10	260
550	Broil	290

index